I0766298

People you Meet

Tales from the Bus Stop

P. A. Barrick

People you Meet

Tales from the Bus Stop

P. A. Barrick

It's human nature to want to showcase our best traits while downplaying those that need work. Some prefer to share a fictionalized or airbrushed story. The people you will meet in these pages all agreed to be as open with me as possible.

<u>**Author's Preface**</u>

People have always made me curious. I understand that almost everyone has a veneer or mask. You may call it a front. When you look at another person, even in passing, you think you may know what they are about by how they are dressed, how they act, how they speak, what job they have, where they live, and so on. What I wanted to do was to show the person behind what you think you see. And I think I have accomplished that.

When I had gotten the idea to talk to people about who they really were, I decided to ride the bus as it is a great way to meet so many different people. I began in Hollywood last summer and as I traveled across the country I rode buses in whatever towns I stopped in and then spent three months doing the same here in Florida when I got home. I met and talked to people from all walks of life as I rode those buses, walked to and from bus stops, waited at the same, and spent time at bus depots and bus stations. I think you may be surprised by whom you learn life lessons from. I often was.

Also note that some of the essays are more first-person and some are more summations of a collection of conversations. This depended solely on the person I was speaking with and what made them comfortable.

I have no formal training in any of the letter after your name pursuits but, as stated, I do have a natural curiosity of people and what makes them who and/or what they are. I also have empathy and compassion for those who have been knocked down. What makes them get back up will always inspire me.

Table of Contents

People you Meet

The White Russian

The Pretty Little Liar

The Free Bird

The Chameleon

The Fruit Picker

The Killer Smile

The Church Lady

People I Met (RIP)

The Statistic

The Streetwalker

The Fallen Angel

The Elder Statesman

SW Florida. We met sitting on the bench at the bus stop while waiting for the 99.

***

Raised in the Lowcountry of South Carolina and in the Gullah culture, his family has always carried that independent spirit. He has continued that tradition.

Although historically, from slavery forward, his family is filled with rice farmers, his immediate family were fishermen. They were mainly shrimpers but also sought blue crab and redfish. This is the world he grew up in.

Small by comparison, his family consisted of his mother, father, and one younger brother. He said he had too many cousins to keep up with and that both of his parents came from large families.

Born the year before the depression started, his life was not particularly affected. He tells me poor is always poor and only rich folks and white folks were affected. His family's life was always the same.

He grew up immersed in Gullah tradition. His great-grandparents, still alive when he was little, had been slaves, his grandfather was also one, but was only two when slavery was abolished. His grandmother was born just after that. The Gullah culture is fascinating to me and we talked about many different aspects of it.

From stories passed down, during slavery the Lowcountry was much different than most anywhere else. Because of the fear of malaria, many slaveowners and their families fled the region in the spring and summer. They left a slave overseer in charge of the rice fields. That is what led to an independent culture and different life for many. Although owned, they had their own community, language, religion and traditions that were practiced in their daily life.

When the Civil War came, and the Union went to secure the coastline, the Gullahs were happily waiting for them. Many ended up fighting with them and he remembers the stories of quite a few from his family that did just that. The Gullahs were also the first slaves freed in South Carolina and also the first to have schools.

He says that even as a kid he understood his life was a little different. For one, his family owned their property as did most of his relatives. His family also owned their boat and had an old truck. He grew up speaking two languages, regular English and Gullah, which is somewhat like an English-based creole. He still has a faint accent.

He and his brother were expected to work and even when young they helped with things like the nets and sorting the catch. Even though education was available, he says that it still wasn't so great and by sixth grade he was done. His brother lasted the same amount of time.

His mother took over then and taught them from the Bible, cultural history, family stories, and life. She was also in charge of the religious life of the family. Although by the time he came along they were mostly assimilated into what would be recognized as Methodist, they still went to praise houses now and then and his mother still visited the conjurer when needed.

When I asked what it was like, he smiles and tells me he grew up surrounded by water and has spent his entire life that way. He described their house as a typical Lowcountry fishing shack. Built very close to the water, it was raised on stilts for the high tides, floods, and storms. He continued that it was small but comfortable and had deep porches front and back to keep it cool. I asked him about living there through storms and hurricanes and he said there were some most every year, but it was just a part of their life. He remembers three big ones. Two in the fifties when he came back from the Korean War and then Hurricane Hugo, which is the one that finally made him decide to leave and come here. I smiled when I told him that just as many came to Florida and he nodded and told me that he thought his present accommodations were sturdier than the fishing shack.

***

When we started talking about growing up as a black man in the Jim Crow south, he had an introspective look on his face, like there were many memories still right there in front of him. He went on the explain, again, that his life was somewhat different and to a degree, the Gullahs were treated more like members of the community. He said he really only got treated like someone lesser when he went into the bigger cities, like Beaufort, and then it was usually by people that weren't originally from there or by those that were unkind anyway. He went on to say that, yes, there were rules and laws you'd better understand, but racism was never overt until he left home and went out into the world. At least in his personal experience.

His first big step out was for the Korean War. Too young for World War Two, it didn't stop him and his brother from playing soldier and war, so when Korea came along, after talking to his parents, he signed up.

Although things were changing by leaps and bounds he says that when he left for basic training was the first time he really understood segregation. First on the train trip there with the separate cars and then around town in Columbia when they got liberty. There were places that he could not go as well as places that had separate entrances or areas. He says that in general, because he was in uniform, once again he was treated a little better overall, but the prejudice came from individuals that had their own problems. He also added that he'd found that's the way it always was and always has been. Even now.

 Although the Army was desegregated, the training companies still weren't. Black soldiers trained together as did whites. He was assigned to the Infantry and his training company would stay together for the long haul. When they finished, he went home on a short leave. He smiled a private smile as he told me about the pride his parents had and how his mother took him everywhere and showed off her handsome son in uniform.

He went on to tell me about the trip to Korea. He said he knew then that he was just a country boy. He knows for sure that he often stared with his mouth open as the train stopped in bigger cities and different places. Being somewhat isolated in the Lowcountry, he said that although he had read about so many, seeing them was completely different. He then shared that the troop ship was as big or bigger than his little town and that his fascination with the world grew as they stopped in Hawaii, a few other places, then Japan on his way to war.

The war itself, like many veterans, he doesn't really talk about. He said it was its own kind of horrible and that he survived it while so many didn't. Two things he will say is that he will always remember the overall kindness of the Korean people he met and the beauty of the country that still showed through the destruction. He was also very interested in the rice paddies. Growing up around rice his entire life, it was interesting to see it from a different perspective.

When he came home, things were still changing. The whole world was. His brother, who had not served because he was married, had taken a leadership role in the family business. He was doing well and now their father was stepping back some and working beside him. He tells me that he was happy for them both and that although the water would always be a part of him, he didn't want to work it to an early death. After he was settled, he went and applied for a county job. He was hired to work with the roads department. He laughs when he says that was its own kind of hard work. He also met the young woman that would become his wife at that time.

Their courtship was brief as both understood they didn't need any time for anything else. His parents loved her and hers loved him. She was also from a family of only two so, as he tells me, they wouldn't have shirt-tail cousins coming out of the woodwork. They were married in a simple ceremony in the church that both families attended. Both planners by nature, they bought a very small house about half way between parents and they settled into their own life in the Lowcountry. She was a schoolteacher and he did his thing. They began building a solid foundation for their life together.

***

At the beginning of our second meeting, he conned me into playing checkers with him. I know I'm a rank amateur but, well, he kicked my butt. Repeatedly. He tried to look contrite but couldn't pull it off. He laughed and laughed. I had been had by a checkers shark. I hadn't even known there were any.

As we started talking, I asked him to tell me about his family. He had pictures all over the walls of his wife, daughter, and grandchildren. He smiled a private smile and told me he was a lucky man. He had found the one and he knew it. Although they had the usual trials and tribulations throughout their years together, they'd had a beautiful life. We talked for most of an hour about his wife, her years of teaching, her care for her students and community, her vigilance in personal empowerment, and her beliefs in right and wrong. She is a beautiful woman and I told him so. He agreed and said she had been the day he met her, and she still was the day she left him. He was quiet as he looked out the window at his own memories.

After a few minutes I asked him about his daughter. He smiles when he tells me that she got a good balance of him and his wife and she was a very serious child and still a serious adult. She's about five years older than me so we grew up in the same era and I asked about her upbringing. He says that raising a black child, a girl, in the beginning years of the civil rights movement and black empowerment was interesting on a lot of different levels.

He remembers when she was still elementary school age, watching as she took on the world. He smiles and says she was just like her mother. I shared that I think there was a little of dad too. He nods and continues that she went to the same school as his wife taught so she couldn't get into too much trouble because it would be known quickly. He also says that she was overall a very good child and grown up from the beginning. I told him I thought that was the case with a lot of only children because they spent as much time with adults as they did other kids. He nodded again and said that she was always a deep thinker and as different experiences occurred that instead of immediately reacting to them, she would take the time to consider all of it and that she would talk to both of them. She grew up with a good understanding of the world and how it worked.

I asked what she did now, and he said that in college she had been a volunteer for many different groups and causes that meant something to her. One of them was the Democratic Party. She has been working with them ever since she graduated and is an advocate. She works with many of the organizations, and others like them, that she volunteered with back in the day, to help integrate their wants, needs, and agendas and match them with candidates that have the same and to overall work within the Party to bring change. I told him that was a mouth-full. He told me that was nothing and that she could talk about it for days. We both laughed.

I asked him when he had retired and what he did at that time. He tells me that he retired right at sixty-five and then had a five-year honeymoon with his wife. I sat quiet then and let him talk. He said that when Hurricane Hugo had hit in 1989 that he and his wife had decided that was enough. Their daughter had moved to Florida many years before and they visited as often as they could. They liked it there and planned to move there when they retired in 1993. In the meantime, his secret fun had always been to buy a lottery ticket when he thought about it. No kind of steady thing, it was just something he indulged in when he had a little spare change. He is one of those people you hear about. He never picked numbers nor spent a lot of money, and with what is now known as a quick pick, he won the lottery in 1992. As he says, it was a lot smaller then, nothing like the outrageous jackpots they have now, but it added to the nest egg they had steadily built and gave them fun money for the first time in their life. That's when they began planning their honeymoon. He also was smart and kept it quiet. Very few knew, and he and his wife continued to work to retirement. When that day came, they put their house up for sale, handed the semantics of it over to a realtor and engulfed on an around the world cruise that would last six months. Since his wife had not traveled a lot, and all of his outside of the country had been back during the Korean war, they decided they wanted to see what they could see. He said it was an amazing time, sharing that experience with his best girl, and that they took so many pictures that everyone was probably tired of seeing them. Then he got up and got out two big photo albums as he and I sat and went through them. Hearing his memories of that trip was beautiful.

Their honeymoon continued until 1998. As his eyes tear, he tells me that was the best five years of his life. They spent all their time together, they got settled in Florida, they took trips when and where they pleased, and they spent a bunch of time with their daughter and two grandchildren. On October eleventh of that year, he went in to wake his wife for breakfast. He always got up much earlier and would quietly putter and watch the early news then make them a little something to eat. She was gone. She'd died in her sleep. He found out later that it was from a ruptured aneurysm. He didn't care why, he just wondered what he was supposed to do now. He was devastated. They had been married forty-five years.

When we started talking again, he said that it had taken him a long time to recover, he hadn't been ready for it but then added no one ever truly was. He had to turn it around and understand how lucky he had been, what a gift he'd had in life, and also be grateful that she hadn't suffered. He knew he couldn't stay in that house any longer and his daughter wanted him to live with her, but he is still a proud and independent man. That's when he bought where he is now.

***

For our third meeting, we are sitting at the small pier of the park beside his condo building and talking while he fishes. He fishes as much to be outside and go through the routine of it as to catch anything. Every once in a while, he cuts his eyes sideways at the attendant sitting about twenty foot or so away from us. He mumbles quietly that he guesses they think he's going to pitch forward and fall in the bay so his babysitter has to come with him. I laugh out loud. He's pouting like a little kid. He looks at me and winks then we keep right on talking.

His place now is very nice. It's a combination. It's a luxury high rise for the retired and wealthy but also offers assistance for those who need or want it. It's a great place and it's right on the bay. His unit is at the back of the building, so it is right on the water and he has a lounge chair on his balcony. He says he has one of the smaller ones because he didn't need much, and he likes it just fine.

He bought it when it was still being built and used to come to this park to fish and watch it go up. He shared that he did get some of that prejudice we've talked when he first moved in. He was, at the time, the only person of color other than some of the attendants and other employees. He went on that some of the white folks were a little trifling and thought he was a porter or something. After a while he just pretended like he was hard of hearing and ignored them. And laughed. He laughed again when they had their first community meeting and some of those same ones were embarrassed when they found out that he was a resident too. I laughed too because he has just that little bit of a devil in him and he gets a look on his face like a little kid sneaking candy when he talks about his misadventures. He says that if his wife were here, she'd give him trouble about it.

He says that although his family was a long-lived bunch that he is very surprised to be here. He never thought he'd be here this long. He is incredibly healthy. Living in Florida, we have more than our share of older people and I've seen so many "look old." He really doesn't. If you didn't know he was ninety, you'd guess way less. I joked with him a little and said he was probably considered quite the catch since there was always about a three-to-one ratio of women to men. He half mumbled again as he said that even the white ladies gave him the side-eye. I laughed out loud again. We started talking then about what he does to amuse himself and, in his case, stay out of trouble. He smiled and said that he now also has a couple of great-grandchildren, so he spends time with his family quite often. He goes on to add that when he's home, if he's in the mood, he'll get involved in the community activities and play cards or whatever. Other than that, he likes the park, and he likes to watch people. And he likes to sit and fish while seeing his memories. Then he looks up at me and says that he also likes a good game of checkers and asked if I'd play again. I laughed as we collected his stuff, roused the attendant, and headed back to his place so I could get my butt kicked again.

My Thoughts and Views

My thoughts are simple. I have a crush on him. He is such a cool person. He is smart, funny, and kind. His knowledge on a variety of topics is spot on and I could just sit and listen to him. His memories are, just like his life is, fascinating, and again, I could just sit and listen. He is a good man in every way. He has a gentle way about him and a quiet sense of humor that sneaks up on you. As he talked about all the gifts that have come to him in life, I understand. Meeting him and sharing a part of his life is a gift I will treasure always.

<u>The Madwoman</u>

New Mexico. In town for a few days, I was coming out of a homeless shelter and she was leaving a municipal building across the street at the same time. She had an envelope in her hand. We gave each other the gay nod and kept going. We ended up waiting at the same bus stop and we began that shallow talk.

That first meeting lasted until the bus came. We were early and had walked to the park behind us and sat on a picnic table. She asked why I was at the shelter and I told her I'd been helping with lunch. When I asked the same, she said she had bonded out on a domestic violence charge. Figuring she'd scare me I guess, I got nosy and asked her about it. She flipped that and was intrigued with the shelter. After about fifteen minutes of talking back and forth, she agreed to be a part of what I was doing. We set a time for the next day, meeting at the same place.

At our first official interview, we started off talking about her background. She is the youngest of two daughters. She says that her parents were both kind and gentle people. And added that her older sister is gorgeous, even now.

I prompted her a little to find where her anger had come from. With that background, it sounded like a pretty good place to be. She agreed. She said that her parents really were pretty great people and neither ever raised their voice, even when the topic of conversation was serious. Her sister, older than her by seven years, didn't either. But she says, she's always had this simmering rage inside of her. She can't remember when she didn't. She felt like she had something to prove or defend.

She said that she was always a tough girl, even very little. She'd fight any neighborhood kid, play any kid game, take on anyone. She says the first time she really remembered being angry was in second grade. Her mother made her join the Brownies and she was not happy about it. There was no way she was wearing a dress. Nope. She said she showed up in her uniform with pants on under it. And stomped in the room, daring anyone to say a word. I laughed. I couldn't help it. She still has a relatively young face and I could just see that look on a seven-year-old.

She said she'd only pee standing up, would only wear boys' clothes, played any sport and played it well. All her friends, except her best friend, were guys.

I asked her if she thought she was possibly transgender before it was something that was talked about. She said no very quickly. She amplified that by saying that she had always thought something was wrong with her and that if she knew she liked girls that must mean she had to act like a boy. So that's what she did. She was too young then to understand that liking girls didn't mean you had to be a boy though she's old enough now to know better.

I asked about her parent's thoughts about it all. She said that she was too young then to even understand what was in her head, so she said nothing. She said when her mom tried to steer her toward more girl-type things she would just get angry and storm off.

That anger continued as she took on the world. She told me that she and her best friend were very much alike. Except in temperament. While she confronted everything, her friend just enjoyed things and rarely ever got mad. She cared about her but didn't understand her.

She says they ended up having sex when they were in junior high. She added that they didn't do it to be girlfriends or anything like that. They did it out of curiosity, something both of them had. She said the experience enlightened her friend, who told her parents all about it. She, on the other hand, liked it a lot but was confused by the way it made her feel. She talked only to her best friend. She told her parents nothing.

Through junior high, her anger grew. She told me that she punched lockers, was a bit of a bully, would storm down halls, and was overly aggressive. Her and her best friend were even closer then, but she still didn't understand her. She said her own anger grew and her friend got more laid back. They both made all the sports teams, they were good, but where she wanted to win at any cost, her friend just wanted to have a good time.

She said over time her feelings grew and by high school, she knew she loved her. She was sure it wasn't reciprocated "like that." Her friend also never hid that she was gay. Not from that first time. She was scared to say it out loud, though it was obvious to anyone who looked. I asked her if she thought her parents would disapprove or what her hang up was. She said they would not have. Although raised Baptist, they were not in any way religious, and they cared about everybody. I asked if she was scared to be ridiculed or harassed. She said no, that she had gotten called a boy since she was little. I asked how she responded. She smiled when she told me she kicked their butts. Though inappropriate, I had to laugh again. I couldn't even help it.

I mentioned that her best friend sounded like she was often her balance and then asked if they were still friends. She quickly answered. No. With that answer, I had to ask what happened. She looked like she didn't want to tell me, so I just stared and raised my eyebrows. She finally said quietly, "Because I just about killed her." My surprise showed, and I told her she had to finish. She said by tenth grade, she was drinking, smoking pot, smoking cigarettes, and acting like a big jerk. Her friend, on the other hand, did none of those things and began to slowly pull away from her and the people she was starting to hang out with. One night she was drunk and got it in her head that she'd teach her a lesson. She was home alone so she showed up at her door, grabbed her by her rawhide knot necklace that she always wore, threw her down in her own front yard and beat the absolute hell out of her. Then she left her laying there, got back in her car, and went home. I asked her point-blank if that was when her cycle of domestic violence began. She looked at me in surprise as I told her that was exactly what it was. Non-committedly, she answered, "I guess so."

I asked if they'd ever talked after and she said no. Her friend was two years ahead of her and there was only a little time left in the school year. Her friend was never mean, she just avoided being where she was. She added that she had never seen her again after she graduated.

***

After her own graduation, I asked what she did. She said she wasn't smart enough for college and didn't want to go anyway. She said her mother's side of the family had always owned an office supply store and her grandmother got her a job there. I asked her if she liked it. She said that she actually did enjoy it. She got to work with people briefly, she enjoyed the small talk, she was more than competent at her job, and she had weekends off.

I asked then when she got her first adult girlfriend and when she told her parents. She said she told her mom first. Right after she graduated. But added that they already knew. She had only been fooling herself. As far as a girlfriend, she still felt the pain of losing her best friend and somewhere inside realized she had no clue how to be a partner in any kind of relationship. She hung around with her new friend, they had gotten closer in eleventh grade, and they went to bars and acted like dummies.

That lasted into her early twenties and even she was starting to get tired of acting like she was still in high school. She decided it was time to give this whole girlfriend thing a try. She took the easy way out and hooked up with someone else she had known in high school. Even she admits they were no kind of match. They just knew each other. She adds that it was always volatile with one being as bad as the other. It ended after about two years when a neighbor called the police on them as they were beating the crap out of each other.

We went back to her job and she said that ended when her grandmother died. They sold the family business to a national chain and she was unemployed. She sat around, felt sorry for herself, and applied for a state job. When she was hired, she knew she'd be secure that way.

Her personal life stayed disastrous though. Although she didn't describe it this way, by what she told me, she lacked the emotional maturity to be in a big girl world. She continued in the bar culture. She went out with women. She is good-looking, and she'd play for a while, but then she'd walk away before too many feelings came forward.

She finally met one worth giving it a shot. She was in her late twenties then and met her through work. She was quiet, kind, and pretty. By the time they decided to move in together a few months later, she was hooked. I asked her how she felt, and she asked what I meant. I said in the day-to-day, how did being a part of a couple feel? She seemed put off as I sat and waited. She said she was stupid. She was often jealous, always possessive, and that would then transfer to anger and rage. She'd scream and yell then storm out and go to her friend's house or to a bar. I was somewhat blunt when I mentioned that she seemed to have had a very good example of how a healthy relationship worked and why was it she seemed to swing the other way? She couldn't answer so I moved on. I already kind of knew what the answer would be, but I asked anyway. I asked when it changed. She said that one night she didn't feel like storming out of the house. She said she got it in her head that it was her place and she'd act like she wanted. She went into a blind rage, trashed a lot of the house and then hit her girlfriend. Then she left. And didn't come home for two days.

She said when she did, she was crying, apologizing, giving all the usual reasons, promising it would never happen again. The girlfriend believed her. Once. When it happened a few months later, she didn't even hesitate in calling the police. That was her first domestic violence charge. She was charged with misdemeanor battery. She pled to a lesser charge, paid her fine, and did thirty days of community service. And her girlfriend left. Smart move.

As she hit her thirties, I asked if she had ever considered getting professional help for her issues. She made a mean face, which I ignored, and then said, "No. Not then." I decided to come back to that and asked what she'd done after the girlfriend left. She was honest when she said she acted like a bigger jerk and went back to her old bar-hopping routine with her same high school friend.

I asked what she thought about herself then and told her not to tell me what she wanted to project, but what she really thought. She said she'd have to think about it before she answered. Which she never did.

I asked her if she had given it a try again. She said in her late thirties she had met another woman she liked a lot. She said she tried to go slower to see if she could get the hang of it and they dated for a long time, spending a night here or there, a weekend now and then, and she was doing well. After about a year, they decided to move in together. Of course, that's when the trouble began. She went right back to her old fallback position and went through her routine in almost the same order as the first time. This time the girlfriend didn't wait. She called the police the first time and she was arrested. Again. And charged with misdemeanor battery. Again. This time they wouldn't let her plead down. She was ordered to court-approved counseling, a fine, and community service. This time for ninety days. And that girlfriend left too.

Talking mostly to herself, she said she was so angry at her for not giving her another chance. Everything was her fault. The bitch. Didn't she know it was a mistake? She started calling her and harassing her and then when she stopped answering the phone, would randomly show up at her house. After saving answering machine messages and documenting times she came by, she called the police again. This time she was charged with stalking. She was pissed. How dare she? The judge, a woman, told her she needed anger management to go along with the rest. She had thirty more days added to her community service, she had another fine, and she added anger management to go with her other counseling. I asked if she had clued in yet and I could tell by the look on her face that she still didn't get it. Or didn't want to.

I asked about the counseling then. She said she sat there with her arms crossed and wouldn't say a word. There was nothing in the order that said it had to be successful, just that she had to do it. I told her that was both immature and stupid. Her face turned red in anger as I looked at her with a blank look. Finally, she said, "You remind me a lot of my best friend." I told her that if she wanted to try and intimidate anyone, that she would need to go find someone else, because I knew what she was running from. That shut her up for quite a while.

I gave her a break and asked about her parents. She said her dad was gone now and had been for about ten years but that her mother was still here, in her eighties and doing fine. I asked what she thought about all this and she said she had never told her. I just shook my head. I don't know her mom, but she seems like the exact person you could and would talk to about most anything you needed or wanted to. I asked about her sister and she said that she was a grandmother and loving every minute. She also added that she had to be one of the best-looking grandmothers ever. She was still a true beauty.

Back into the hard, I asked her about present day and why she was walking out of the jail carrying an envelope. She said that she had decided to give it another try when she hit fifty and it had worked out the same as the rest though worse this time. She had really hurt her girlfriend and had been charged with felony battery. Thinking only of herself, she added, "It won't get lowered either. Because I'm a repeat offender. If I get convicted, I'll lose my job, And I'll get jail time." As I sat and listened, I had not one drop of pity for her. She had enough for herself anyway.

***

That was the end of our conversations and interviews. I felt the need to talk to her on a personal level after we were done though. We spent almost two hours together as I talked directly to her. She didn't like a lot of what I had to say, but I know she heard it all. I made sure she did. As we were getting ready to leave, I took a moment and whispered in her ear. She looked shocked by what I told her as I got up and walked away. However, it's something that is private, and I will never share.

My Thoughts and Views

She is, without a doubt, the most emotionally-stunted person I have ever met. And she is that way by choice. By continuing to live an immature, selfish, and shallow existence, she is disrespecting herself and anyone that cares to get to know her.

She is confident in her outside world. However, as a woman, she completely lacks self-confidence and self-esteem. She is emotionally immature. As with any child, when she doesn't know how to properly express what she is feeling, it comes out as anger.

It is a copout and the easy way out. By not committing to growing and evolving, she has a childlike belief that she can then not be held responsible for her actions. However, she is an adult, and has found that is not true.

It's a pity too. She had a very solid background that was open to conversation and understanding. She chose, at an early age, to trust no one but herself. She thinks it keeps her safe and hidden, but in reality, it shows who she is.

She is also somewhat homophobic. Somewhere early, she picked a role to play. That is acting, it is not real life. She has never wavered from that beginning, though she is grown.

It's all sad, honestly. You can tell by talking to her that she has the capability to be a pretty cool individual. All of her best traits are flipped and are also her worst. She has made the choice to remain that way.

Domestic violence is a veiled secret in the gay community in general. It is not spoken of often enough. In the lesbian community specifically, the percentage is almost double. If you are like her or with someone like her, seek help and support. It's the right thing to do.

<u>The Nightingale</u>

SW Florida. I met her when I woke her up. She was sleeping on the bench at the bus stop for the 7. I wanted to sit down so she had to at least sit up.

***

That first time I met her was actually about two-and-a-half years ago and I've always talked to her on and off since. She's not stupid, not at all, she's just high most always.

Since she agreed to talk to me for this, she's been the highest I've ever seen her, wasted really, and I've seen her through some pretty rough times. She shows up as promised at our scheduled times but is so high that although I talk to her for a few minutes, nothing of substance can be discussed. I understand that she's scared. I get it. But, at our last meeting I told her that she had to be somewhat straight if she wanted to continue, that she was wasting both of our time, and I would have to move on to the next interview. She promised she would.

***

She was sitting on the deck over the bay when I walked up. I said, "Well?" We talked for a couple of minutes to see how she was doing and she seemed focused on what we were trying to do.

In her former life, she was a nurse, an RN. And she tells me that's where all her problems started. That's not completely true, but it flows well, or so she thinks.

Raised in Oklahoma, she was the daughter of evangelicals or bible-thumpers. As she adds, "Bible-beaters really." Being an only child, they focused all their energies into making her right with the Lord. Of course, their views were extreme and rigid, and the way they tried to do that was to instill fear, guilt, and righteousness into every single thing she did.

The way she looked, acted and dressed was scrutinized constantly. She was told who she could associate with, where she could and couldn't go, what she could read, watch and listen to, etc. Every single part of her life was regimented. She was in God's Army. She shakes her head when she repeats that.

She said she never knew when or if she was doing something wrong. It depended on the day and what amount of crazy had overtaken them. I asked her about the ways they tried to mold her, and she said, "Let's see. I'll miss some, probably a lot, I'm sure. Bible study. A lot. If that didn't work, standing Bible study. If that still wasn't getting the result they wanted, a switch and more Bible study." She looked up then, "Sometimes they just beat me to get the devil out of me. And it's funny, I was actually a good kid. I didn't sass, didn't run around, didn't do much of anything other than what they told me to.'" I asked her how she had to dress, as we had grown up in the same era, and as she went through and told me about jumpers, wrap-around skirts, middy and maxi dresses, modest shirts and shoes, and all the rest, I could visualize how she looked when she was younger. She finished by saying, "Definitely no pants of any kind. Those were for men."

We moved onto her schooling and she said that when she was younger, elementary school, she went to public school with all those godforsaken people, poor people, black people, trash, degenerates, and the rest. She still shakes her head. She explains how much they disliked it but there were few options, then adds, "But you can believe most every day when I came home, I was washed in the blood of the lamb."

When she started junior high, a proper Christian school opened, and she was sent there. If she had thought home and church were bad, school was like a combination of both plus she had to learn as well. She told me that she didn't realize until she got away from them and went to college that much of what she had been taught, particularly history, was completely wrong or seriously skewed. I asked her about other kids that she went to school with. She said most were like her, cowed and scared, but there were a few hell-raisers too and she was told to stay away from them. She said, "You have to remember, my graduating class had forty-two people. It isn't like a big school like you'd think. If I remember right, kindergarten through the end had less than three-hundred kids total. All white too." I asked her where she graduated, and she said safely in the middle of the pack.

We talked then about college. Her parents had wanted her to go to a church-based one and over a years' time she convinced them that to get into a good nursing program, she'd have to go to a better school. She finally won them over. I asked her how she felt, and she said, "Scared. And free. For the first time in my life."

She said at first, she was a little wild. For her anyway. She ate all kinds of things she had never been allowed, met all kinds of different people from all kinds of places, made friends, and also had her first drink. She added, "Looking at me now, you'd think I liked it. But I didn't. Not the way it smelled or tasted. And I didn't do it again until much later." By her sophomore year, she had another first. A boyfriend.

Unknown and never spoken of to her parents, she was shy and nervous, but was learning to enjoy being a part of a couple. There was no way they'd ever approve. And he was black. She just shook her head. "Definitely didn't say anything about any of it to them." She lost her virginity at the age of twenty and also mentioned that she didn't particularly like that either. With a sad look on her face, she added, "Seeing what I do now to myself most every day and by choice, you probably wouldn't believe it. But I like it even less now. I know why. Because I'm selling myself for drugs. It's not a loving thing. It's definitely not any kind of relationship, other than a business one. Really, it's mostly terrible." A tear rolled down her face as she finished.

Even with all the new in her life, she did well in college. Raised to have her life structured, the class routine helped her keep to a schedule and she enjoyed it. Still socially uncomfortable and shy, she was slowly gaining confidence and expanding her circle. She says that she was usually surprised when new friends complimented her. That was something she definitely had never heard and wasn't used to it. She told me her time at school was a great bridge for her. She had time to transition from a rigid world into a bigger view of the reality of her choices and who she was. She started knowing herself a little, she was making friends, was learning so much, and could envision her future. She looked at me then, "This is not what I ever envisioned for myself."

Her relationship with her parents became distant. The more they pushed to keep her in their world, the more she pulled away. She told me it took a while to see that she was becoming angry. It wasn't in the forefront but after she'd talk to them on the phone or get a letter, it would rise up again.

As school was coming to an end, she had a ton of options. She knew she was never going back to Oklahoma, so she considered the various places offered and picked Atlanta.

***

After all the school, after all the clinics, after all her hard work, when she started her first job she fell in love with nursing. The staff, the patients, the hospital, all of it. She had made the right choice and was so happy. For fifteen years, she loved every day of it. Then she got hurt.

She hurt her back moving a patient one day and was prescribed a lower end pain pill. It helped a little but didn't relieve the overall pain. When she went back for her checkup the next month, the doctor gave her something stronger. Those worked. Much, much better. Not only did her physical pain go away, but all her other issues did as well. She got to feel nothing for a while. And she fell in.

***

She told me that it started off slow. She only took them when she got off shift. It didn't take long until the one became two. Soon after, it was one about an hour before she got off work and then that became half of one when she got there. After that, it just snowballed. And she began running out way before it was time for a refill.

One time only, her doctor fell for the spilled it in the sink routine, but he wasn't the type to just go along. She had two work friends that each complained of pain once and got prescriptions for her when they fell for similar lines. Both were uncomfortable and told her they wouldn't be able to do it again.

She went doctor shopping then and began asking people at work who was the best to go to, then slowly weeded out the ones she knew she wouldn't be able to get over on. She found the one she was looking for and took him for a long ride. She actually rode him until she was let go from the hospital. She had lost her way and those pills became her only focus. She said she barely even realized she had lost her job.

She was no longer in any kind of contact with her family and had slowly isolated herself from any close friends or relationships. She had nothing to fall back on and knew she had to work. She ended up getting a job much below her skill level in a nursing home. Once she had the routine down pat, she began stealing the patient's pills. She was smooth enough in the beginning to not get caught. She would give them half of what they were supposed to get and take the rest. About a year in, the quiet complaints to administration started coming in. Not too long after, she was let go. She had lasted barely a year. They told her they would not prosecute if she turned in her license. At that point, she didn't care anymore anyway. She said she remembers the flip thought of whatever.

Since about six months after that, she has been on the street. That's about eight years right now. She liked it at first. No one knew anything but what she told them. She could get a lot higher for a lot cheaper. Everybody else was high too so there was no judgement or concern, only when they could get high again and who they could get it from.

She had a teeny bit of money still. Believe it or not, she got unemployment for a year. So, those first six months on the street were like a honeymoon for her. Even with her previous life, her lack of street smarts, and her constant high, she had enough sense not to let others catch on that she had any kind of money anywhere. She said she wasn't that high.

When that last stipend ran out, she did what she had to in order to get what she thought she needed. She bummed a bit and that was cool since she had shared before. But eventually she wore out her welcome and had to earn her own. She was to the point she'd never imagined she would be. She began selling herself to get it. She looked at me as we were finishing for the day and said, "I still wake up sometimes and wonder how it happened."

***

Although she can be eloquent in thought at times, she is mostly full of shit about her current circumstances and choices. I think she still sees glimmers of who she used to be, and in those times that her thinking is clearer, tries to pretend that's still who she is. I can't figure if she's lying to herself or lying to others to try to convince herself. Or both.

A few months after I first met her, she used to sleep behind the bushes of this business about a block from my house, my dog and I literally tripped over her. When I talked to her that day, she said that she had to get ready for school and had to pee on the way to catch the bus. Even my dog had looked at me and shrugged. I had played along and asked what she was going to school for and she had told me that she was working to get her CSN license. That was also before I had known she had been an RN in her other life.

Over time, I would see her here and there in different situations and she would give me the same story or one similar, I just nodded along since we both knew it wasn't true. Often as she told the story, she was so high she could barely stand up, but she did wear scrubs while saying it.

Since she agreed to the interviews, I have been much more direct with her about her various classes, schemes, truths and lies, and asked her bluntly to tell me what's really been going on with all that since she hit the street.

She has been in detox and then various programs nine times. Because she isn't stupid, she can talk the talk when she needs or wants to, and she is always given a chance. There are a lot of programs here that will help someone that wants to help themselves. I think she has worn out her welcome with all of them.

She actually has been in three programs involving nursing. And she really was in the CSN one. For about two weeks. The other two were for aides or assistants. She lasted about the same amount of time in both of those. She has also been in five programs for non-medical pursuits. Those run the gamut from unskilled manufacturing to basic data entry. The one that she was in until two weeks ago was the only one that surprised me. A large cellular phone manufacturer out-parcels their repair work. I think most people know that. But she, and others in programs like hers, are the ones they get out-parceled to. I'm no kind of paranoid but it seems that a drug addict with a history of creative livelihood would not be the top choice to be working on other people's phones. But no matter, she got kicked out of that one too.

I asked how many times she had been in jail and she couldn't tell me. It has been that many. But she has had both misdemeanor and felony convictions. Even if she was able to walk away from her current life, she could never work as a nurse again. She is now a convicted felon.

My Thoughts and Views

My thoughts varied some because, although she is overall a nice person, I didn't like her. I finally understood why.

She has an incredibly high level of denial of her world now. She also takes no responsibility for the choices she continues to make. By being intelligent enough to get in these various programs that she does, she is taking a spot from another that may be ready to change their life.

She, on the other hand, is not ready to change hers. She has no acceptance of any part of it. She is too smart for her own good in this case and I believe it often becomes a game to see what she can do instead of an effort to accept help and do the work needed to find her way back. If she eventually makes that choice, she will be a success. But she has to take that first step. Alone.

The Seoul Man

Arizona. We met on the 7. He was letting his daughter drive his car to school for the first time and this one stopped at the mall where his store was.

***

He was another chance meeting for me. When I introduced myself and he told me his name, I said, "Anyo Haseyo, Adashi." His eyes lit up and he smiled. He said everyone just assumed he was Chinese. And. Talked. Very. Slowly. To. Him. He laughed, and I did too. He asked where I had learned, and I told him I lived in Korea for quite a while. He said, "Funny. I've never been."

He is an American, born and raised. His parents immigrated here a few years after the Korean War ended and he grew up in California.

He was born when his parents were a little older. They were very traditional, and he was an only child. Although spoiled some, his upbringing was very strict by American standards. When first grade came, his parents were almost forty whereas his school friends' parents were in their twenties. Their entire culture was Korean though they embraced the freedom of America and were very happy to be a part of it all.

He said that for most of his childhood he led what he felt was two lives. His traditional one at home and his American one while at school and with his friends. He is also bilingual and speaks both languages easily.

He was raised to succeed in school, in life, in family, and as he got older, in college and eventually in his career.

***

Although he liked some sports, he was a techie from a young age. He was excited by the future world and what would be possible as time passed.

I asked him how that had related during school and he laughed and said that he was an AV geek, a band geek, in the Science club, the Chess club, and on the Debate team. I asked him, with a straight face, if he wore high-waters too and he laughed out loud.

He excelled all the way through school and graduated second in his class, but he was secretly fostering an alternative outlook. Business success, making money, and other outward signs of success didn't really interest him. As he was fascinated by the burgeoning tech world, he was also fascinated by the alternative music scene. That was his joy.

***

He was accepted into a very good school and his major would be a double, Computer Technology and Computer Science. He was in Nerd Nirvana.

All through school he had played the cello. He had transitioned that and taught himself to play bass. The underground music scene in California at the time was huge and he immersed himself in it as he did in school. He and some friends formed a band and began rocking in one of the parents' garages. He tells me that they were actually not bad and by his sophomore year, they had started signing up and auditioning for open mike nights around town. He even got two tattoos. On the top of each wrist. In Korean, one says heart, the other says soul.

I asked how his school world was doing during all this and he said that it was all great and he was happy because he was maintaining the balance while enjoying his two favorite things.

He was stimulated completely, and he said the four years went by at light speed. Again, he had done well and graduated in the top fifty, which was a huge achievement at such a large school. His parents were ecstatic.

I asked more about them including who he was most like. We talked about the kind of people they were and their personalities and outlooks for a while then he said he looked like his dad and acted like his mom, but really, he had gotten what he thought was a good balance of both.

Before he had even graduated, the recruiters and headhunters were all over campus. Tech was exploding and they were looking for the best and the brightest. He was both.

He took a job with a start-up in Simi Valley that had an outlook much like his own. His parents were overjoyed. He was too.

***

He said for a solid year, he never looked away from his work. He was into every single aspect of what they were doing and couldn't get enough. He even worked when he didn't have to, often wearing earphones with his music blasting in his ears. He said that way he still stayed connected to both. He laughed and said when he stepped away at the end of that first year, his ears were ringing, and his vision was blurred. He shook his head as I laughed too.

He decided then that maybe he should work on getting a life. In the traditional way of Korean families, he still lived with his parents but that seemed a little ridiculous to him and he got ribbed a lot as he tried to explain it to his friends and co-workers. He went in search of his first place.

He knew he wanted to be near work but also close to the music scene. He is overall detailed and a planner. He took his time until one really struck him. Then he jumped on it. He said it was super cool too. He found a loft not far from either, in the old industrial section of the valley. A developer had bought a warehouse and redone it. He said he loved his place and that is was very much who he was. He settled into life as a young adult, though the first people he had over were his parents. He giggled like a kid as he told me of their first reaction to the area. They were wide-eyed and wary as they got in the elevator to go up, but they just nodded in their quiet way and then approved his choice.

***

He said that year two found him still working hard but starting to branch out some. They started working open mike nights again and it was a great way to let off steam from his work week.

Then he smiled. When I asked him why the grin, he said that it was near the beginning of summer and they had just finished a gig at a coffeehouse they had started playing often. He said he had just taken his bass off and was leaving the little stage when a gorgeous woman approached him and asked him to have coffee with her. I laughed now because he still blushed when telling me the story.

He said that she was like a goddess and for once, he could barely talk. He said he remembers little, other than sitting there like an idiot as she talked easily and asked him questions about himself. He figured he must have given good answers because before he knew it, she asked him if he would like to go to dinner with her the next night.

He said he felt like a moron. This beautiful woman had asked him out. He never would have had the nerve and really, things like that didn't even cross his mind most of the time.

I told him that he was a good-looking guy and I didn't understand why he didn't think a beautiful woman would approach him. He said I didn't understand. When he said gorgeous, he meant Gorgeous. He felt like an unsure kid whenever she spoke but somehow managed to say yes and remember where and when he was supposed to be.

By the time of his date the next night, he had managed to get it together some. He showered, fixed his hair, picked a proper hipster look, and rolled his sleeves up a little so his tattoos would show. He stopped and bought one simple daisy, he didn't want to overdo it, and walked to meet her. He said when he walked in, he smiled. The night before he had been overwhelmed but when he saw her and then really began seeing her, he realized that she was the one. He just knew. He said when they were taken to their table, he pulled out her chair, bowed, and handed her the daisy, then sat down and started talking. He said they never stopped.

***

He said that although his parents were surprised that she was not Korean, they grew to love her as much as he did. A year later, when he asked her to marry him, she said yes. He was so happy and so was she. So were his parents. And hers.

They incorporated his family's Buddhist traditions with her family's Episcopal ones and had a completely modern wedding seaside. She had daisies braided into her long blonde hair. They were barefoot. It was at sunset and his band played through it all. He says that he knows everyone says it, but she was the most beautiful bride ever and he was overcome. After the ceremony and reception, they were off. They honeymooned in Seattle and saw as many bands as they could in the week and a half they were there.

They settled into his loft and continued working hard. She worked in advertising and was a talented graphic artist. He continued his path at the start-up and then on the weekends, they dove into the music scene together.

***

As they started heading into their late twenties, they decided it was time to start a family. They both loved the loft but thought that probably wasn't the greatest place to do that, so they went on a hunt for their first home. Again, taking their time and being thorough, after about three months they went to see this cool little bungalow. They looked at each other and said yes at the same time. They signed the papers that day.

A little over a year later, his daughter was born, and he was in love all over again. She was a beautiful child in both spirit and appearance. She had all his Korean features with her green eyes and blonde hair. She was a peaceful and happy baby. And, she was never anything but daddy's girl.

So, their family became three and their social world opened further to include activities for her too. She loved the music though. He said she had a good rhythm from the start and would often pat her hands or stomp her feet to it as she got a little older.

***

Then his light went dark. When his daughter was almost four, his wife began not feeling well. Like him, she was never really sick unless she caught a seasonal cold or something like that and they were both alarmed as she continued getting sicker.

By the time they went to the doctor, it was really too late though they tried to focus on the positive, not the negative. She was diagnosed with stage four pancreatic cancer. They tried to put a good face on it, but they were both devastated.

He said both of their families stepped up big time then. His parents were getting older but loved their only grandbaby and loved his wife. Her parents felt the same but watching their daughter disappear was tearing them apart. He said that she obviously quit working but that he also took a leave. It was time to focus only on them and their daughter. There wasn't a single thing that mattered more at that time.

His eyes water when he talks about that time. He said the best word he's ever found to describe it was heart-wrenching. For everybody. Their daughter was young enough that she knew Mommy was sick but didn't understand more. He was losing his best friend, his partner, his soul mate, and his rock. But she was losing her life. He said that whenever he wanted to be sad or feel sorry for himself, he had to remember that although he was losing so much, and it was terrible, she was losing everything. And there was nothing he could do to fix it.

Four months later, she was gone. Just like that. He wanted to just step into the darkness, but he couldn't. He said if not for his daughter, he probably would have joined his wife. He isn't being dramatic when he says it either. He said whenever he was losing it, all he had to do was look at her. She knew something was wrong, she didn't really understand where Mommy had gone. He said whenever he would cry, she would pat him and say, "Don't cry, Daddy. It's okay. I love you, Daddy."

He picked up his second joy and let the music help him heal too. He went back to the cello some and would play complicated sonatas and concertos to help organize his mind but also to allow him to feel. He said when he was angry, he would pick up his bass and bang out the hardest rock he could. He said between his daughter's love, his family's support, and his music, he made it through. And he'd never thought he would.

He never went back to the start-up. He just couldn't leave his daughter then. He also knew then that he couldn't be in that house anymore. Everywhere he looked, everything he touched, was a memory.

His company stuck with him though. They were his friends as well as his co-workers. After an appropriate time, when he was beginning to come out of the fog, one of the heads came by to talk to him for a while. Although the visit was personal and he wanted to make sure they were doing okay, he also had an offer. They were going to be expanding to the southwest. They needed someone that knew their way to head it. They also understood that he wanted and needed a change of place and space. After talking it over with his parents and his daughter, he said yes. They were moving to Arizona.

***

That was eleven years ago. He only stayed with the start-up long enough to fulfill what he felt his commitment was. He said it was about eighteen months. His daughter was so young, and he didn't want her to grow up in daycare. His mother and father came and stayed with them for about nine months to help them transition to a different way of life. And to spoil their granddaughter more. He smiled a little bit when he said that.

During the end of his time with his company, he thought about what he wanted to do. Still a planner, he decided to focus on tech for the everyday person. He worked out a business plan for himself and then he made the rounds of senior centers and other organizations to teach computer technology to those that had been left out of the loop.

Although he doesn't say it this way, I do. Because he is personable and intelligent, because he knew what he was doing and how to convey that to others, his business did well from the beginning. He says that the people he taught felt comfortable with him and when with an older crowd, he always thought about how his parents would learn. Because of his music, he was comfortable talking in front of people and he hit that edge of cool that made him relatable to younger crowds. He taught during the day while his daughter was in school and if he ended up with a night or weekend class, he took her along as his assistant. The older people loved her, and those his age were amused. Until they realized that she was as smart as her dad. Then they were impressed.

She is sixteen now and reminds him more of her mother every day. She has memories of her but not a solid understanding of who she was. I asked how she was doing, and he said that his biggest deal right now was letting her drive the car. Then he made a terrified face as I laughed out loud.

He has transitioned mostly into repair. He likes to putter. That started from his classes too since not only did his students not know how to use them but didn't know what to do when something went wrong. He had started fixing them then.

Recently he has gotten back into his music, just in the last two years. He met some people one night when he and his daughter had stopped for a bite to eat and after talking for a while, was invited to come to one of their practices. He said he felt rusty, but he fit right back in the groove and it felt great. He now has time to play a gig now and then. With his daughter's approval.

I asked him if he ever considered dating again and before I even finished, he was shaking his head. He said that even though it is on him, that he knows himself well enough to understand that he would always compare them to his wife and not see them for the person that they are. He is still grieving all these years later. He said his heart was broken when she died, and it still hasn't healed. He's not sure it ever will.

My Thoughts and Views

In a world often filled with those comfortable in shallow waters, he prefers to delve into the deep with all its complexities, colors, and surprises.

He is still excited by his career. When he transitioned from straight tech into teaching, he gained that depth by sharing what he loved with others.

His music has always had that level. From an early age, he learned to put all of himself into the soul of it. By doing that, he shares those same feelings with those who hear him play.

His traditional upbringing taught him depth of understanding. He grew up thinking things through patiently. He is a quiet philosopher who embraces what he knows to be true.

His relationship with his wife showed him the deepest love then the deepest pain. The love for his daughter helped him understand the meaning of the first and heal from the second. Although he sees his wife when he looks at her, I see him as well. Like he had told me about himself in relation to his parents, she has a good balance of both of them.

As far as his choice to live his life alone, I understand that it is the right decision for him. When you meet The One, that love lasts forever, whether they are still with you or not. She was in his heart from the first day and she still is. I think she always will be.

<u>The Pretender</u>

Virginia. I was hanging in Carytown in Richmond and so was she. We were both waiting for the 78. We started bullshitting a little bit and both decided we'd just wait for a later bus. We meandered to a cafe with outdoor tables, sat down and started talking

***

She was so engaging that one of the first questions I asked her was how she thought others saw her. She told me that it depended. In her earlier life, probably a globetrotting, English-teaching, backpack-living, young American woman. Since then, a few different things. She added that then and now, it depended on whether you knew her in daily life, or if you worked with her. If it was the latter, you saw someone doing a superior job.

Always intelligent, observant, and able to fit in anywhere she chose, she grew up very independent, self-confidant, and somewhat aloof. She was always very direct, even as a young person, but she could throw bullshit when she needed or wanted to as well.

Her growing years, she keeps very private. Even now. Just from the little things not said, it was privileged but not healthy. She avoids any direct questions about it, saying it was okay, and leaving it at that.

Through school very quickly, she was still young when done. She went and talked to an Army recruiter about what she wanted to do. Not knowing her, they gave her the usual blah, blah, but her brain was her secret weapon. When she was sent to take the ASVAB tests, they thought there was a glitch somewhere or maybe somehow, she had prior knowledge. But no, she was just that smart. She was fully and heavily recruited then. They wanted her to be an officer but she wanted no part of that. She was sworn in as a PFC instead.

She went to Fort Jackson, SC for Basic Training. Without trying hard, she was Top Troop with double expert, top class rankings and an impressive PT score.

She was then sent to Fort Huachuca, AZ and the Army Intelligence School. She was at the school for a year, training in a couple of different areas, but her time in service would be undercover. It was perfect for her and for them since she was comfortable in any situation. She was an E-4 or Spec 4 when she finished up. One thing they did at the completion of her training was to legally change her name. One of the reasons she had been chosen for the assignment was because she had no close ties or connections. Although she had no immediate family, they just wanted to cover all the bases. She had no problems with it, she didn't like her name anyway. It also had to be one not related to anyone she knew, so she ended up using the last name of the legal clerk that did all the paperwork.

Her first (temporary) assignment was to go back to Fort Jackson as a PFC and get sent through AIT there. This was basically a test to see how she'd do with living two lives. Her assignment was to watch the interactions between the instructors and students and to report anything abnormal. She says it was interesting to see the things that did occur. Some she had figured she'd see and others had surprised her. She didn't elaborate on any of it though. During this training period her contact person was back at Fort Huachuca. She was there for three months then she went back to Arizona to get her set up for her real assignment.

She would, for the most part, be on her own after that set up period. It had to be that way since she would be completely undercover for the duration. As she was done with everything, she was given a cash payment to get herself set, some general guidelines, and then sent on her way. She was headed to South Korea however she chose or found to get there.

She would have someone in Seoul at the US Embassy as her contact so she had to make her way there first to meet them and let them know she had arrived. After that meeting, she really was on her own. She could only contact local military bases in an emergency. She had a set protocol. Her reports would be hand-delivered by her to Seoul once a month. She would go over it verbally and be briefed on anything she needed to know at that time. If there was anything that needed immediate attention, she had ways to contact them that she had memorized.

Otherwise, she was a young American, living on the Korean economy, and teaching English. That's how everyone knew her and, really, that's who she was. Just the other too. And very, very few knew that.

Her job was to observe and report. Her focus was military personnel and illegal activities. Things like pharmacies, and selling of cigarettes, Class Six (alcohol) or PX goods to Korean nationals. Really, everything off limits or out of the ordinary. She was to listen to all talk and gossip.

She got to know everybody. She befriended neighbors, merchants, waitresses and anyone else that would carry on a conversation. She says that she enjoyed that though since she liked talking to people anyway. Her personality really was the right one for what she was doing. Although it was an act, it wasn't. It was more like a duality. Around town and around her neighborhood, her face became commonplace, which was the point, as she watched the world around her.

She learned quickly that the hookers knew everything. She knew all of them anyway and many had become her friends. Not only did she get a lot of information, but she enjoyed playing with them and ended up spending a lot of her time doing just that.

She lived a normal life while there. She loved the people and the country, so it was no kind of hardship to be there, though her job description considered it just that. She decided she would stay as long as they let her. She made sergeant in six months.

All her Korean friends thought she was a globetrotter too. And she was. But much of her travels were involved with her work. She covered Korea many times over, and the rest of the Orient almost completely. She also had trips to Egypt, Guam, Australia, and Hawaii. When she got on the trail of things, she was told to follow.

Living two lives most of her life anyway, she had no problem adapting to any place or situation. She loved what she did and enjoyed herself immensely. She spent four years and five months in Korea.

She went back to Fort Huachuca for her last month. She was there for out-processing, debriefing, etc. She was also there to get paid. And it was going to be a lot. In her six years, because she was essential, she had never taken leave. She got paid for those one hundred and eighty days. But they also said that she had never officially had a day off in that time and was paid for five-hundred-and-seventy-six days as essential personnel. She had also never gotten her military pay once she went to Korea. She hadn't needed it because she did fine with her English classes and this was before direct deposit. She was paid for fifty-three months. She also received her TDY (temporary duty) pay for all her travels. Her salary had always also included Separate Rations and Basic Allowance for Quarters. Last, she was also reimbursed for much of the travel stuff she had paid for herself. It all ended up averaging about two thousand dollars for every month she was in. She left the military after six years with a check for one hundred and twenty-five thousand dollars. She had also agreed to stay on inactive reserve for six years. It was a month before her twenty-fifth birthday.

***

After that, her life got really interesting. Yes, even I laughed when I wrote that. She went back to the Orient for a year on a personal quest. She tells me that it was the smartest year she ever spent though she won't say why or where. But, when she made it back to the states, she went back to her love. Food. She took a junior executive job with a large hotel. She loved the work. A lot. And the people. She says she was there only a little over four months when she met a person that would change the course of the rest of her life. She refuses to elaborate but that same individual is still an important part of her life now, thirty years later.

***

I will mention that you can probably tell that she is a woman of multiple layers of secrets and information not shared. Between the childhood she won't discuss and her military service, she is very adept at sharing only what she chooses.

During that same period, she became involved with a woman that she still calls her only true love. More like star-crossed lovers, although their time together was short, that woman is the one she still holds dear to her. As a sidetrack, I asked her if she knew where she was now, and she told me that she had found out that she died a couple years back. She looked off and away as she shared that.

Back to that period though. Her life continued on a normal path, or her normal, and soon after their time together ended, she went back to school, culinary school. In rapid succession after its completion, she then moved to Europe and then continued her life's pursuit of wanderlust. After that start, she lived in a lot of different places and with a lot of different women. She covered much of the east coast before she came back home for a while. And that was only the rest of her twenties. She also told me (very) brief stories of some of those women and experiences through it all. Even though she is often serious, she can make you laugh through it all.

She grew up, again for her, at thirty. She met a woman and settled into a life. They complemented each other and had many different businesses over their years together, which they both enjoyed. Though she was often uncomfortable in "normal world" she managed since her, by then, wife had the wanderlust as well. It lasted fifteen years. Until she got sick.

Then her world flipped upside down. Confronted with too many things at once, she freely admits she completely lost herself for about two years.

***

At our last meeting, I got her talking a little more openly. I asked her more about her illness as a starting point. She was honest when she said that it truly threw her for a loop. She had always met life head on and conquered whatever needed to be conquered to keep moving forward. She said that not only had she been completely stunned and caught off guard by its sudden onset, but she had been devastated as well.

She shared some with me but only after agreeing that I wouldn't write about that part of it. What I can say is that through that turn of events, I'm surprised she is still alive. I'm not sure I would have made it.

She actually agrees with that assessment and is also surprised she is. She went on to tell me that there was no one there to fight, there was this unknown entity killing her and for the first time in her life, she was confronted with something bigger than her. Without even knowing she had done it, she gave up.

She tells me that she really was lost for about two years and truthfully shouldn't have lived through them. When I asked her what happened, she said she woke up one morning and realized she was in big trouble. Then, a truly big deal for her, she said she needed help to win. Admitted it. And got it. That was the true beginning of the acceptance of her new life.

***

Somewhat laid back or melancholy, or a little of both, I got her talking about much of her life being someone else. She said that even when she was her, she wasn't. That so much of her life had been surrounded by falsehoods that the transition to her job in the military had been an easy one. She likens much of her world to a show that her ex had told her about. It was called The Pretender. Each week the main character became a different person and did different things. She said that resonated with her. Hers was somewhat different because she was always herself, but she took on different roles throughout her life depending on the circumstances surrounding the period. I shared that was a hard way to live and she said that honestly, it was her normal and sometimes a lot of fun. Sometimes, it was also a necessity for survival. She didn't elaborate on that either.

***

To end our time together, I moved the conversation to her present-day life. She says that these last eight years have been spent in reflection. She still travels all over. She still bullshits as much as she is real. And she still enjoys her life just the way it is in whatever incantation that is at whatever time. When asked if she'd change anything, she shakes her head and says no. Not a minute of it.

My Thoughts and Views

This woman was a tough one for me. I guess because she is so many different people, I had many different thoughts. She is actually pretty cool all around. She is funny, smart, self-depreciating, and has a good understanding of herself. Because she has spent her life all over, she also has an honest and balanced outlook of the world and of the people who inhabit it.

<u>The Bitter Pill</u>

New York. We met on a long one in Manhattan. She was the driver and I was the only passenger early on a Sunday morning. We had over an hour to spend together so I struck up a conversation.

***

The first thing I noticed when we started talking was that she speaks in a monotone voice. She also rarely speaks at a higher volume. At first I thought it was because she was focused on driving. Later, I found out that wasn't the case.

She is a New York girl, born and raised. She is ten years older than me and is the oldest of two. She has a younger brother. Her parents are gone now. She grew up just outside of Manhattan itself. She still lives there in the same house she grew up in as she inherited it when her mother died.

After a twenties of doing a little of everything, she landed the bus driver job. She's been doing it ever since. She actually hates it but it's secure so she stays. She has one year until she retires and she told me that she counts every day.

As I hopped around different subjects looking for one that would connect, each brought negative replies. She seems to hate most everything and her bitterness shows behind her controlled voice. There was a reason for that too.

She was raised as a hardcore Catholic and attended Catholic schools. She tries to joke but doesn't quite make it; she is a recovering Catholic. I understand that religion can be a polarizing topic but her anger toward the church is deep.

I decided that maybe a different setting would help her tell her story more openly so we set a time for the next day to meet at MOMA. It's one of my favorites. We spent the rest of the bus ride in shallow and light conversation. I'd find out more during our next meeting.

***

The first thing I realized is that she is a big chicken. She hides from commitment. That's to most anything or anyone. Instead of putting herself out there, she wears a mask of cynicism and bitterness. She thinks it makes her look witty and smart. It doesn't.

Since I had gotten her talking a little bit about the Catholic church, I decided to start there. She told me that her parents were very much into the church. That is how they lived their life and there was no question that she would follow on that path as well. It took a while until I found the core but eventually we got there. When she was six, her birth father started touching her. She was terrified and didn't say anything to anyone. It took almost three years before she did. She told her mother. Surprising her some, her mother believed every bit of it. This was in the early sixties and a woman's place was a woman's place. Her mother was a tough one though. She went to the priest and talked about what was going on and wanting to get a divorce. He counseled her that her place was with her husband and he wouldn't give his or the church's blessing to break her vow. She says her mother was really surprised, and then she was pissed. She kicked her husband out of the house and filed for divorce. There wasn't even a question that it would be granted. But, and the big one; it was her mother that was kicked out of the church, not her birth father.

Molestation of a child is terrible in most any way you can imagine. Although it never goes away, you can heal emotionally. A good friend of mine was molested for seven years before she told. She had nightmares, acted out, had an eating disorder. You name it; she did anything she could to try to make the pain go away. It finally started to when she started talking about it. I was always proud of her for standing strong. She told me she realized that by talking about it, she was helping herself and hopefully helping others. Unfortunately, I've known too many with that experience and I understand what it does to you. Obviously, everyone is different, but similar patterns do show too. Back to the present though. That's where her anger started and it's grown since then to encompass every part of her world. She holds it tightly to her instead of learning to let it go.

About a year after the divorce was final, her mother met the man that would become her stepfather. After a bit, they decided to get married. She tells me that so many were surprised when her brother was born eight months after they had but she knew how to count too and understood they got married because they had to. Her mother had converted to Episcopalian after getting the boot from the Catholics and they had a church wedding. She was the flower girl. It all worked out no matter how it started. They were married for over forty years until his death a few years before her own.

She is actually well-read and intelligent but she uses that as a mask too. Using that same voice always, she'll discuss anything she's read with you. It is in depth and boring. When you step around the book, she pulls her mask back up. That happens with most anything. She'll expound on big picture stuff, always taking the cynical view of whatever it is. Unfortunately, that is boring too. Really, most conversations are.

I finally asked her why she speaks the way she does. I asked her if it was practiced or natural. Because her voice doesn't change, it was hard to see her surprise and anger when I asked. But it was there. She told me that she was always somewhat shy. In a book she read somewhere, it said that if you speak quietly, it makes people focus and listen. That's true to some extent, but I told her that within that you still had to have a modulated voice to show emotion and feeling when having a conversation. I asked her how she expressed anger. She looked perplexed and then told me that she didn't ever get angry though sometimes she was disappointed. I laughed.

Her biggest achievement in life is to be a Lesbian. Not gay, queer, homosexual, or any of the others. But a Lesbian. Although the word has been around for a while, it really came into regular conversation in the 60's and 70's during the women's rights movement. She says that in the same voice too and talks about both movements, blah, blah, blah. When it was obvious that I stopped listening, she mentioned that I was one too. Yes, I am most definitely a gay, homo, queer. But I'm not from Greece. I also understand everyone has different preferences on defining themselves. Her way is her way; my way is mine. To annoy her or make her laugh, I asked how many pairs of Birkenstocks she owned. I laughed as I could tell she was counting in her head. Although she'll talk about both those movements until your eyes bleed, she's not really committed to them either. She is detached but informed.

Carrying that over, I asked her about relationships. She's had none that really lasted. She had a couple that she just stayed because it was there. Again, the lack of emotional commitment shows after a while. However, being a true Lesbian, she is friends with all her ex-girlfriends, their new partners, and anyone else involved. She is not currently in a relationship. I asked if it was possible that I could talk to any of them and she gave me the number for the one she lasted the longest with. I wanted to hear another perspective about what I was observing.

***

My second meeting was on the phone with her next to last, ex number three. She lives in another state now and they were together for eleven years. I asked her to tell me whatever she'd like me to know. She said they met in a women's bar in Manhattan one night in the early nineties. I guess the one they were in had like a lounge area that was quieter. She said she wasn't really a dancer and was just relaxing and enjoying different conversations when they met. Because she is a schoolteacher, she said it was nice to talk to someone that was well-read. That was the hook that caught her as through the evening, they discussed many different ones. They decided to meet a couple of days later at a potluck that was happening. I started laughing and she did too. She said, "Don't say a word." I was still laughing. She said that at first it was nice to be dating someone that was intelligent and seemed very woman-focused. They discussed the various movements, different musicians, and a bunch of other stuff too. I asked her if she had caught onto her voice yet. She said that she kind of did and kind of didn't. In the places they met and went to, it seemed more like she was speaking that way to keep their conversations private. She said she didn't realize it was an all the time thing until the first night they spent together.

As we talked more, she told me that it took about six months to understand that she was an emotionally absent person. Seeing much of the same things I did, at first she just thought she had a calm nature. She said their first fight was an eye opener. I asked why and she said that she had gotten really angry about something and was venting and banging around like you do and that she just sat there and stared at her with what could best be described as pity. Like she was sad to see her lose control of herself and too bad she wasn't like her. "I even know that sounds bitchy. And I felt bad after too. But the more I thought about it, I realized my reaction was normal and hers was off. Because she didn't have one. But the worst part was that she really did have one. If you looked into her eyes, it's like you could see all the turmoil behind them but her exterior just showed that fake sense of calm." She said it was a few months later again when they had an almost true argument. She had actually done something that irritated her. Instead of talking openly about it, first she pouted and when she kept questioning her, she became passive-aggressive. "It was like once she let it out, that's how she was about half the time with me."

She told me that it always started like a cold arrogance. More like she was looking down on her for having emotional reactions. Pity, like she had said before. She went on to tell me that she had to easily be the angriest person she had ever met. And it took a while to understand that too. Because she had been wearing that mask most of her life, she was adept at hiding behind it. She thinks the only reason that she saw it was because they lived together. She added that if they were just social friends that saw each other once in a while she doubted she'd see it.

She named her the watcher in her head. She said that behind that dry intellectualism, she was actually very socially awkward and if just trying to have a regular conversation, she would often say something inappropriate or crude. Because of that, no matter what was going on, what the discussion was, whatever, that she always sat a little back from it, detached and watching. When she felt comfortable with what was being discussed, she would then join in and bore everybody. I started laughing again.

I asked her about the eleven years. She said it wasn't really that long, more like eight, but it was too long. She said they went out for about a year before they moved in together. Around the fifth year, they bought a house. She said it was a cop out and she knew it, but she mainly stayed because of the house. The dogs loved having their own yard and it was a nice house too but by year six, they had separate bedrooms. She figured being physically absent was no worse than being emotionally absent and she just started doing her own thing again instead of trying to tiptoe around the mood swings. She also said that technically, to end it, that my interviewee had cheated on her. Although she was detached, she was one of those people that didn't like being alone. To bridge the breakup or whatever, she went out and found another before she left. When she did, she moved in with that one. She adds, "Yes. I knew her too. But I don't tell tales. She would have to figure it out for herself instead of me sounding like a bitchy ex. They only lasted about two years. I don't think she's gone out with anybody since then." I told her that she was single. "It's too bad. She has some good traits but all those years of pent up anger affect every part of her life. I doubt she'll ever change."

We talked for a little longer and she told me that if she knew where ex number two was, that would be the one I needed to talk to because she'd always told her that she was the love of her life. She gave me ex number one's phone number and told me she might have a different view since she was her first and added that they were still friends, etc., etc. I laughed again and thanked her.

Ex number one and I talked for a while but it was close to a carbon copy of my conversation with ex number three. She also mentioned ex number two but said she'd have no idea how to find her. I figured at least I had a starting point to our next conversation.

***

I decided to go backward first this time. I asked her to tell me about her parents. Very abruptly, she told me that she had never seen or talked to her father again once her mother kicked him out and she didn't consider him a parent; she considered her stepfather her dad. I asked her to tell me about him and her mother. She said though her mother had mellowed some with age, she was always either angry or bitching about something or someone. She never remembered a time that she didn't. She added that at the same time, she was still a traditional housewife. Although she worked, she still held that traditional role. She said that at the same time, two things that opposed that stood out. She was actually very funny and had a great sense of humor. The other was that she absolutely loved Christmas. Everything about it. And it was always a big deal in their home. When she moved onto her stepdad, she said that he was probably the angriest person she had ever met. Like her mother, most anything could piss him off and he'd rant and rave for hours and days sometimes. Always going on about something as he strutted around. She added with him that even with all that, he was a good provider and would defend his family to the death. She went on to tell me that her brother was probably the most normal of all of them.

I jumped forward to ex number two then and told her one and three had both mentioned her. I asked her what was so different that had made her stand out from the others. She actually smiled. She told me that she wasn't like them. I asked what that meant. She told me that she was younger and had a completely different outlook on life, she called them earthy crunchy dykes and she said and did whatever she wanted whenever she wanted. She also added that she wouldn't let her get away with any bullshit. She'd call her on it every time to make her be real. She added that she was a complete and unrepentant pain in the ass, couldn't care less that she was, and laughed at them all the time. She continued that she was probably the most intelligent person that she ever knew but not any kind of bore with it. She used that like she used everything else, to just enjoy life. She didn't worry about things, didn't stress over mundanities, didn't get fired up about crap that didn't matter. She finished by saying she was laid back and ridiculous. I asked how long they were together and she said she wasn't sure, about two years. I asked what happened and she said that she had gotten tired of her negative energy and filling her up. She told her that she needed to learn to do that for herself. She ended it by saying, "After that comment, she turned and walked out the door. I've never seen or heard from her again." I asked her what conclusions she had drawn. She told me that she got sad, then she got mad. She learned nothing. She decided to just stick to what was safe and easy and pushed the rest away. She never budged again.

To close out our time on a positive note I asked her to tell me her favorite thing in her personal life. She said that she liked to do anything that was woman-focused; potlucks, tea dances, music festivals, game nights and those types of things. She said that she always enjoyed those quite a bit. I then asked if she had a favorite thing at work. She laughed and smiled. She told me that when she could see somebody running for the bus, she'd wait until they got about even with her and drive off. Then she laughed and laughed.

My Thoughts and Views

I actually did this one last. I let it sit for about a month and would re-read it now and then to find a different view. I even made myself really focus to see if I was overly harsh. The realization was that I had not been. I couldn't nice it up or gloss over anything else. Like her third ex told me, she has some good traits; you can see them if you really look. But I also understand that her mask is no longer a mask; it's a part of her now. Her home life was angry in almost every direction you looked so that was her example as a child. But, she moved out when she was eighteen. And she's no longer a child. In the intervening forty years plus, she had plenty of time and space to work to change her view or ask for help in doing it. The people she has connected with throughout her life focus much on the inner person so most anytime she could have put her big girl suit on and been honest about the feelings she had. She chose not to for reasons that are her own. Since she prefers not to delve deep, I was unable to get any response on why she made that choice. She has chosen to keep herself detached, yet still a part of her own life and those of others.

The Believer

Louisiana. We met at a bus stop. We were both waiting for the same one. Our conversations began as we rode all the way to a local grocery with the best produce ever. She was riding the bus because she is politically correct. She'd really rather not, but she thinks that's part of who she's supposed to be.

***

Born outside of Vancouver and spending her formative years between there and Washington state, she grew up in a logging family as the younger of two daughters. She was quietly insecure and grew more so as her family moved from place to place to place.

The first thing she shared that really struck me is that when the new forest was chosen and after a road was cleared, her family's house or cabin was then brought in by helicopter. As the head of the company, they always had the same home, it just moved with them. Every time I think of that, I see Dorothy's house in The Wizard of Oz, spinning through the air until it landed.

After our first conversation that day, she invited me to come to a nearby Buddhist center. She works there, and as I found out, lives in a communal setting with some of the other staff. She coordinates all the business operations and also works with their programs for volunteers, classes offered, and other things of that nature.

She is committed. There is no doubt about that. But her eyes have that unsettling shine to them as she talks about her world and her role in it. To me anyway, it seems like an almost desperate need to belong. Somewhere. Anywhere. If you talk to her at any length, or know her a little better, you may feel she's too enthusiastic or a bit of a phony.

She came to the center about ten years ago. It was in a different place then. The current center opened not long ago, and she is comfortable there. She has her life just so. She likes to be in control of herself and the people and world around her. It makes her feel safe.

She gave me the tour before we sat down in the garden to talk. She started to explain what everything meant but I stopped her and let her know that I already understood the symbolism, but I thanked her for the thought. We chatted for a few minutes about this and that and then I steered her back to her earlier years.

I asked her first how she went to school, moving around so much. She said that it was sometimes dispiriting and with her already shy and insecure, it just made it worse. She added that it was somewhat like what circus kids endured but for longer periods. She also said that because many of the woods were in the same general area, she often came back to the same ones and at least knew some of the kids and teachers. She mainly went between the Vancouver and Bellingham areas with stops at a few others thrown in. She said the biggest difference was going back and forth between the American education system and the Canadian one. I asked her about that too and she said because she was born in Vancouver, she was considered a Canadian citizen, but she had been a US citizen now for longer than she was ever that.

After school, she headed off to college, also in Washington. She majored in English because she had not a clue what she wanted to do. She already had control issues and by that point they were starting to hit the lower rungs of OCD. She had to keep order in her mind and surroundings otherwise she could be thrown off for days.

She met the guy that would become her husband while in college. He was a man's man much like her father. She says that looking back, it was a wrong pick, but at the time and place she was, it seemed right. They fell into a carbon copy of her parent's marriage. Already somewhat independent and outspoken over big picture thoughts and ideas, the inner her could never balance with the person she was trying to be. She said their marriage was unhappy, stressful, and they didn't really have a lot in common, but it was safe. So, she stayed. He cheated. He was domineering. She was passive-aggressive and snarky. Not great all around.

She told me only one good thing came out of it. Her daughter. And that had made the rest worth it. But her husband left her, which she had never even considered, and it put her in a deep tailspin. She didn't know what to do. So, she ran. Taking her daughter with her.

She ended up at a Buddhist center in California that would take her and her daughter in. That was unusual, but they must have sensed her desperation. She started out as a volunteer, living on site communally with all her and her daughter's needs provided for. Through her time there, she became completely immersed in the belief. She became almost arrogant in her devotion. As with every other part of her life, the need to fit in and feel safe and secure led to the rest.

As said, I have no question of her commitment or devotion. It's not an act. It is an intrinsic part of who she is. All or nothing. Black or white only. Gray is way too uncertain for her. The other is rigid and she likes it. She is safe.

But, the part of her that she runs from is the real her. She is funny, intelligent, pretty, and a great conversationalist. But that almost manic need for the rest constantly pushes that part back.

I asked her why she eventually left California to come here and she looked uncomfortable. I stayed quiet as she fought with herself to be truthful.

She told me that she liked to be in love. Whether it was a person, an ideal, or a movement, she loved it or them with every part of her. Whereas someone else might meet someone and maybe show some interest, she says that if that happened to her, she equated that interest to falling in love and then it went back to her all or nothing pattern.

What happened in California was that by that time, she was one of the bigwigs and part of the permanent staff. She started poaching volunteers. Usually male, but she had met a woman and although she had never experienced that, fell head over heels. She did this quite a few times in her six years and whispers were starting since everyone that she had connected with ended up leaving the program after that infatuation ended. A couple might not have been noticed, but six stood out. She went into meditation for three months to try to understand and came out with no answer. Eventually, although she was a huge asset, they could no longer dismiss the other, so they helped find a place that met her needs.

***

I asked about her daughter and she is in her late twenties now and living her life. I asked about their relationship and she was honest and said her inability to stop micro-managing everyone and everything had harmed it some. It got better when she realized just what she was doing to others, had a long talk with her daughter, and apologized. She said that lucky for her that her daughter is a pretty terrific kid and having watched those actions her entire life, understood and accepted the apology. She also said their relationship now is pretty fantastic, probably because they don't live near each other.

While we were on family, I asked more about her parents and her sister. She had only mentioned any of them very briefly. She says that her and her sister are opposite sides of the same coin. She mentioned that they even look a lot alike and that they were always close because of their moving around so much when they were younger. Her sister is outgoing, funny, bawdy, and intelligent. She is very much her own person and doesn't pretend to be anything but her. She admires that though she is afraid of it. She says that she loves to hang out with her and live vicariously through her. I just raised my eyebrows with no comment.

Her parents are traditional. Her father is an American, raised in a rough and tumble world to be a man's man. He has the swagger, the attitude, and the belief that the man rules. She said when she was younger it was overwhelming because, even though all chimed in, his word was final, no matter what the situation was. She adds that he is good-looking and strong. He was raised in the timber business and was made to know all the jobs associated. He grew up working the woods. She both loves and fears him. He is in his eighties now and still rules the roost.

Her mother was June Cleaver. She is Canadian. She was raised to be that person. She tells me that some of how she acts is how she saw her mother growing up. She goes on to tell me that her mother is smart, artistic, pretty and funny. And that often that wasn't seen as she accepted her role and lived her life that way. She said that she and her sister used to have secret mom time where they went out to museums, and as her father said, engaged in numerous other frivolous pursuits.

***

Back to leaving California though. She came east. The woman she'd had the affair with was actually near here and for a brief moment she thought she'd like to rekindle that. She says that she realized what she was doing though and stopped herself from contacting her.

Here, she is a bigger fish in a smaller pond. She definitely knows how to work every part of her world and does it with confidence and happiness. She also likes where she is. Professionally. On a personal level, she admits that if she's willing to commit herself, her healing can really begin. Seven years older than me, she is just beginning to allow the real her to emerge and to believe that's a good thing.

***

It's a sunny Saturday as we sit in the garden again. I wanted to try and talk about more personal stuff today, so I started with her last statement from our last meeting. I asked her what she meant by if she was willing to commit herself. She seemed surprised as I just sat quiet and waited.

She said that she had seen a psychologist for a long time, but it didn't help. I asked if she'd been honest or told him what made her look good. Surprised again, she said it was more the latter. I commented that she had wasted two peoples' time but at least the shrink got paid for it. Then I asked her what she was so afraid of and she said herself.

I stared quietly again as she explained that she had never really known who she was, that she had spent much of her life being what she thought others wanted her to be. I added that made everyone happy but her and she agreed.

She talked about her intention with immersing herself in Buddhism, which she did, but that outside considerations always pulled her to be the not real her. I asked her if she didn't think she was good enough and she said probably not.

I took a few minutes to tell her about the real person I saw and how cool she truly was and mentioned that fake her was a pretty transparent cover. I finished by telling her that she was a chicken. She laughed and shook her head as I smiled.

We talked about her times in meditation, but she said she was still thinking about what others thought, about how she appeared, etc. I told her she had more value than that and prodded her to consider a period of silence in a more monastic setting where she wouldn't be around anyone to impress but herself.

We went back to when she first realized what she was doing and though she said it had most always been that way to some degree, that when her husband left her, it had floored her. She had been good, she had played the role she was supposed to, and she had catered to his needs. I asked how she felt about it all. She said first she was confused and didn't understand at all. Then she was mad, but not at herself. She blamed anyone and everyone else. The she was saddened and felt she had no value to anyone. I told her she had to have value to herself.

And she does. Professionally and with other experiences for the collective good. But from a personal standpoint, she doesn't really. She also thought she was getting too old for all this self-realization, but I chimed in that every day had something new to learn, see, and do. I also added that every person went only at their own pace, not by a clock, and to quit selling herself short and being such a chicken. She laughed out loud at my bluntness. Then we sat and talked about all kinds of things to end our time. It was nice.

My Thoughts and Views

She does what so many seem to do. She distracts herself from herself with outside stimulus. That way she can avoid knowing. In her case though, she actually runs from it. She covers her flight with a sheen of devotion. She thinks that keeps her safe.

When I told her the real her was a good person, I wasn't kidding. If you can break her out of her self-imposed imprisonment, she is all the things I described.

She thinks it's too late to change, but I know it's because she's afraid to try. And to know. When I think of her, I think of gray. She needs to find it. She needs to embrace it. She needs to live it.

The Solitaire Player

SW Florida. Although I had seen him around for about six months, we officially met one morning as we were sitting on the bench at the bus stop waiting for the 6.

***

He is a single older man that lives in a waterfront high rise designed specifically for older people on a fixed income. He follows the same routine daily. He is quiet and keeps to himself unless engaged by others. I've always joked that I often act like an older man, but with him, it was true. It's my grandfather's fault.

I had already, in my head, named him The Prince.

He is actually eighty-two. He both looks it and doesn't. He is a widower and lives in the tower across the street. Reserved, he doesn't speak unless spoken to. I, of course, am the opposite. We were a match made in heaven. He chuckled lightly when I said as much as he is far too polite to just tell me to shut up.

***

For our first official meeting, we sat on one of the benches in the garden outside of his building. As I am a World War Two history nerd, I found his story fascinating. He is a war orphan. He was brought to America before we were even formally in the war. His family was killed in July in the first Blitz campaign against Great Britain in 1940. At the time, Britain was planning evacuations of children to keep them safe. Though some were sent to the country, many were also sent here. He was sent here with one of the earliest groups. He said all he really remembers is being sad and being scared. He was only four.

He does remember understanding that this would now be his home. Later, he understood that those who had parents that survived the war were sent back to England. He was already an orphan and he was sent to live with a couple in Connecticut. They became his parents and New England is where he grew up.

He says that looking back, he could tell they were worried about him for most of the first year. He seemed so solemn and sad. They loved him as much as they could, made him a part of their family and community, and slowly, with the resilience of youth leading the way, he came out of his shell and embraced his new family and new life in America.

He said that his accent faded a little each year and now you only hear it faintly when you get him talking. His reserve has stood the test of time though. He has remained quiet and introspective his entire life.

***

His first love was the sea. He said it always attracted him and admitted he felt the romance of it. His family was comfortable and he spent his summers seaside. He still remembers his first boat. It was a 1952 ALCORT Sunfish. He smiles when he says that he loved that boat. He said as the years went by, he became more skilled and worked with bigger boats, eventually piloting the family sailboat, but that he always kept his Sunfish. He only sold it about six years ago. I'm sure whoever bought it was ecstatic since he told me that it was still in great condition.

He says that it was completely natural that when he graduated, he joined the Navy. It was the year after the Korean War ended, the true beginning of the Cold War. After his training in Norfolk, he was assigned to the brand-new carrier, the USS Forrestal. He said they were busy from the beginning. Not only were they a training ship for airmen and a show ship for dignitaries, but they also supported the Suez crisis and other things needed in the Mediterranean. They often went to port in Mayport, which is in Jacksonville, Florida, and that was his first time in the state where he now lives. He said their main base was Norfolk. He talked for quite a while about all their adventures as well as his own. It is very obvious that his six years, all spent aboard the Forrestal, were a great period in his life.

However, it is Operation Strikeback that he remembers above all else. In 1957, they took part in a gigantic NATO operation in the North Atlantic. Their port was Southampton. It was his first time setting foot in Great Britain since he had been taken to America seventeen years before. But it was a big deal for more reasons than that. You see, he met a girl.

***

Whenever he had shore leave, he went to see what he could see and to also, kind of, feel his heritage. He didn't drink alcohol, so he often found a bookstore, library, or a nice park. In one of the shops he frequented, he met a lovely girl. Much like him, she was introspective and bookish. He says now that it's a wonder they ever had a conversation. But they did. On the third or fourth trip there, he got up his nerve and asked her to tea and she said yes.

He admits now that he was starry-eyed. She was beautiful. She was intelligent. She was more than he could ever have dreamed. Because he was not there long, they became pen pals. Everything they could not verbalize, they said in the letters they wrote to each other. He says this is how they learned everything about each other. And that is also how they fell in love. They wrote letters for a little over two years, until his time in service was done, then he went back to get her. She said yes then too. He still has the letters.

They were married in England. His family came over and hers was happy because, really, he was British after all. After all the paperwork necessary was done, they came back to Connecticut together. They lived with his parents while they settled in. He enrolled at the University of Connecticut in the School of Engineering and she found a bookstore, much like the one she had left, and settled down happily in the world of books. He said those were idyllic years for them both as they planned for their future.

When he received his degree, he was hired by General Dynamics. Not only was he a Navy veteran, but he had done well in school. Their main focus was as the builder of submarines for the US Navy. They were headed to Groton. He never left. He worked there for forty years.

***

As we began our second conversation, we started talking about family, I asked more about his parents first. He told me that they were just good people. It was that simple. He said they were kind and gentle, even his father, and that they were well thought of outside of the home too. They were active members of their community and were involved in quite a few pursuits involving that.

I asked him to describe them for me. He said his mother was a true beauty, inside and out. He remembers that first year and her gentleness as she tried to help him feel safe and find his way. He said that never changed. She wasn't a voice-raiser, she was the kind that would take a minute to think about things and then talk to you about her thoughts. As far as physically, she was a woman with auburn hair, on the tall side, faint freckles that you couldn't see when she was wearing makeup. He added that she only wore it for social responsibilities, she didn't really need it nor like it. He said that she was funny and artistic and a lot of his favorite memories of her were when she was just being silly. He said that happened a lot. That she never took herself too seriously and he could remember times at the water when it would be her and him building intricate sandcastles and then both taking pleasure in jumping on them and smushing them after.

He said that throughout her life that really never changed. She always had a secret smile just for him. They would have dinners or whatever with many guests, but she would look at him sideways and either wink or roll her eyes. He said that continued, for the most part, until the day she died, well into her eighties. He adds that he loved her very much.

With his father, he started off telling me that he was the more reserved of the two but could still have his fun too. And that he had gotten his love of sailing from him. He said most of their one on one time was spent on the water as he showed him the fun of boating while teaching him the semantics of it as well. He also taught him maritime rules and history.

He was an engineer too, but in his case, he had been a civil engineer and had worked for the state in his career. He told me that he was up in the hierarchy and that went from the time of the development of the interstate system forward. He added that his favorite part of his job was in developing bridges. He looked at it as art to create them in functionality with the nature around them and the roads they served. He had also lived well into his eighties.

All of them were bookish and over time they discussed most every book. He added that his parents were also very good about allowing him to read what he chose, including banned volumes. They thought restricting any art was the job of the family, not the law. I told him I would have liked them a lot. He agreed and said that as he got older and started making school friends that his house was often the gathering place.

***

We went back to his married life then. I knew he did not have children and asked if that was a conscious decision. He said that it had been a little of both.

Because he had been older when he finished college and embarked on his career, he and his wife were already a unit. They enjoyed each other's company, they went to movies, theater, art openings, traveled, as well as many other things that interested them.

He was almost thirty when he started at General Dynamics and she was just a year younger. They talked about it some because at the time that was an expected part of life's continuity. Grow up, job, marry, kids, live life, retire, die. I laughed and said I didn't realize he was a secret cynic. He told me on that subject, he definitely was some because it was one area where many had bad manners and thought it was okay to intrude in their personal business.

But his point was that they liked their life as it was. Neither cared personally. His background we know but his wife had also been an only child. He added that they did find out later that they could not have children. I asked about adoption since his had been such a great experience and he said they talked about that too, but in the end said no to that as well.

***

I asked what they had done then, and he said they went on a fifty-one-year honeymoon instead. Then he smiled. He added, somewhat slyly, that they eventually had kids, just a different kind. When I smiled back, he said they'd had Corgis. Lots and lots of them. All named after royalty and it was Queen Elizabeth's fault. He thought that was funny and began chuckling.

Just after they bought their small house in Groton and got settled in, they had them. Usually two, but sometimes three. They had gone to a dog show on one of their first excursions and had really liked them. After the show, they spoke to the woman that had shown hers and soon they had Elizabeth and Philip. I told him that was ridiculous, and his eyes twinkled. He went on to say that they were great dogs and that theirs were probably spoiled, but they were also very smart. They took them most everywhere they went throughout their life. His mother had grand-doggies instead and spoiled them too.

I had to do it, so I asked all their names. He said, of course, Elizabeth and Philip were first in 1965 and from then to 2011, they'd had ten. The others were Charles, Anne, George, Henry, Grace, Catherine, William, and the last was Diana. As a sad ending to that discussion he added that his wife had died in August of 2011 and Diana had only lasted about a month longer, older and despondent over the loss of her mom.

***

For our third conversation, he invited me to follow him home after our morning ritual.

His place is very small, an efficiency. Apart from his sleeping area, what space is there is filled with books and photographs, an armchair, and a small television.

We spent our first hour looking at his life in photographs. They ran from right after he arrived in America to the first months of 2011. He talked and shared stories of the pictures he showed me. I could feel his life as he did. One of the last of his wife, he saddened and said, "Alzheimer's. It's a terrible way to go."

In the early stages, she was often frustrated and angry. Her entire life had been inside her head and in her books and her art, yet she often couldn't remember even the simplest work. He said in the end though, they sustained her. Where by then, she usually couldn't remember anything in the present, those stories soothed her. He wiped the corner of his eye and cleared his throat as I sat quietly with him.

***

Another I had to ask came next. I said that with the long career he'd had as an engineer and having no children, adding that he didn't seem the frivolous type, was his wife's illness the reason that he now lived in fixed-income housing? He nodded and said it was. He would have spent everything, and almost had, to make sure she was taken care of and comfortable. He didn't particularly care how he lived because she wasn't here with him now. And then he smiled sadly. We sat and talked quietly for a few minutes then he got up to get the letters he had told me about.

My Thoughts and Views

As an engineer, his work was meticulous and exact. It had order. His daily routine has those same qualities and gives him purpose, a connection to the world, and something to look forward to each day.

Where many think he is lonely, he isn't. He is alone. I think from a lifetime of intellectual pursuits, he is happy inside his own head. His life is in his memories of the past while he continues to move forward on his solitary journey.

As mentioned, long before I got to know him, I had named him The Prince. It turns out that I was right all along.

<u>The Constable</u>

South Florida. In town for two weeks and wandering, we met first at the downtown bus depot. It is within his patrol area. Because of a decent-sized homeless presence, he spends a lot of time walking and talking to them and others. Since we are both chatty we struck up a conversation one day.

***

He grew up in a completely normal world in Pennsylvania. His mother was a teacher and his father had a white-collar job in the mostly blue-collar textile industry.

It was a small town, he was a jock, and Friday night football was a big deal as well as social time for everyone. He was popular in school and was on the student council. He had above average grades. Basically, he was a big fish in a small pond.

When he graduated, he joined the Army. The ASVAB testing he completed pointed him toward the Military Police. He was excited and thought he would really like that.

He first found the dark side when he was stationed overseas. He can't say if he was influenced by others, but he takes responsibility for his own choices.

He told me that it started when they busted enlisted people for petty things. Since that would be at the very least a Counseling Statement and could be an Article Fifteen, he looked at it as helping them out since the actions were from stupidity not criminal enterprise. He began trading different things for not busting them.

That ended up expanding and carrying over to prostitutes. He began taking blow jobs for their exoneration. He says that he was often cruel to and with them. He, even now, shows some shame but he still continued doing it.

I asked if he felt powerful or powerless. He thought about it for a minute and answered, "Both." He went on to explain that he felt some anger and powerlessness in the beginning because he had always kind of been "Top Dog" and now he was in a foreign country with a language he couldn't understand, he was just a PFC, and he wasn't popular like he had been in high school. He admits that he was confused as much as anything.

He has emphasized, more than once, that he still did his job, did it well, and liked it. He says that he felt he had found what he was meant to do. He pushed thoughts of the other back though he continued to engage in it.

That side started at the age of twenty.

***

He met the girl that would become his wife when he was home on his last leave. They hit it off immediately and he went back for what was his last six months in. They spoke most every day.

As they grew closer, they both decided they really didn't want to live in a cold climate anymore, so he began applying to police departments in only warmer places.

Outwardly, he was exactly what those departments were looking for. He was handsome in that typical white boy way, his military record was very good, he was fit, healthy, heterosexual, and motivated.

He told me that he ended up going for interviews with five that he had applied to and chose the one he is currently with after his interview, and a weekend spent with the department where he did ride-a longs and met many of the other officers.

***

He took a month off after he got out and they got married during that time. A perfect beginning to a perfect life.

In rapid succession, he became a grownup. He was married, had a mortgage, bills, and a myriad of new responsibilities. He said that he was proud that he had handled it well.

About ten months after they got married, she was pregnant. As that progressed, he made excuses for himself to indulge again. He didn't see it as a betrayal, only as his need.

As a rookie, he was just doing patrol. The area he was assigned hit a lot of the areas the homeless frequented. Just like regular folks, he got to know people by face and some of the troublemakers by name. It didn't take long to get who did what.

***

He's now been with the department for twelve years and he is a sergeant. Over the years, he remained on patrol. He didn't try to move to other departments because he wanted to be there as much as possible for family events. With his shift changes he still misses things, but he knew that in some of the other departments, with call-outs and whatnot, he would have missed a lot more.

He is now assigned to the same area that he started in. He is still doing the same things and often doing them more now.

His daughters are ten-and-a-half and eight. His wife went back to work when the youngest started school. She works in the cafeteria there and is still on the same schedule as they are. He says she's happy because she gets adult time and also has the girls.

Since he is already cheating on his wife and has broken his vows to her many times over, I asked him point-blank if he ever thought about his daughters when he was engaging in his extra-curricular activities. He seemed surprised and somewhat mad. He said no. I pushed some more and pointed out that in a few short years they could be put in the same position as those kneeling before him. He seemed shocked and had most decidedly detached himself from the reality of what he is doing.

After a few quiet minutes, he quietly said, "I've never looked at it that way. Not once." I asked if he had taken the humanity out of the women he uses, and he just said, "I guess I have." At that point he seemed sad rather than mad.

In a worst-case scenario, that could be one of his daughters one day. We talked more about the women in the street and I pointed out that they were someone's daughters too and that I was sure their families never imagined that for them either. That ended our conversation that day.

***

Our next conversation started out contemplative. I asked him why the serious face and he said that he had been thinking about our last conversation. With no prompting, he told me that he had grown up in an Episcopal family, but it wasn't beat over their heads or anything. It was more a once in a while and holiday thing. He continued that they had always done so many family things on the weekends that they often weren't at home. Somewhat abashed, he said that he sounded like a flake or something, but his family now had a more spiritual lifestyle as opposed to an organized religion-type life.

I stayed quiet as he continued. He told me that over the years, as he started having a hard time with the things he did, he would go to a Catholic priest he had met. I asked if confession helped and he said, with a smirk, that it obviously didn't stop the behaviors but that he usually felt better for a while.

I asked him if any of the officers he knew did similar things and he said that he didn't think he should speak to what anyone else did or didn't do. I went back to his family for a while. He laughed and said his parents were now officially snow birds and that his brother, sister, and their families came down to visit now and then but that he didn't go back to Pennsylvania too much. His wife's family also comes down a bit and they now have an official guest suite for all of their visitors. I asked if he had a good relationship with all of them. He thought that he did but added that her little brother was a pain in the ass.

***

The next time we spoke was somewhat light (and not). We talked about the criminal element he had dealt with over the years. The serious, the good, the bad, and the ridiculous. I laughed through most of those stories and told him he could have his own gag reel with the ridiculous ones. Then we both laughed.

Our next topic was about his sometimes want to leave law enforcement. He is back and forth with it. He thought that being away from the influences would make him stop the behaviors and engaging in them. He thought that on his bad or weak days, when it was right there, it was easy to give into his impulses. He stopped mid-thought and said, "I want you to understand that this isn't an everyday occurrence. I've gone many months at a time with it not really crossing my mind." He also added that wasn't justification nor an excuse, but he didn't want me or anyone else to think he was some kind of freak. I stayed quiet as he continued. "I really do think about leaving but when I look at the word ex-cop, to me that sounds worse than bad cop. I feel like people would see my application or resume or whatever and wonder why I couldn't hack it. Especially now, since I could retire in eight more years." I asked if that was fear of the unknown and he admitted it probably was to a degree. He talked about the security of his job and what that did for his family. I asked if he and his wife had ever talked about it and he said they had. He added that although she obviously didn't know some parts of it, they both had the same thoughts on job security and other family concerns. "She's great though. She told me she'd support me in whatever decision we came to." Then he just shook his head sadly and said, "I suck."

***

After a surprise text, I walked to meet with him. He was smiling when he pulled up beside me. He was off-duty and wearing regular clothes and driving his personal car. I told him his legs were really white. He laughed and said that he didn't think poly-blend was conducive to tanning. I told him he should transfer to the bike cops. He shook his head and said, "No way. I'd be dead in a day."

After some light chit-chat, I told him that he seemed perky after his pity party last time. He told me it was my fault and laughed. He said that other than his priest friend, I was the only one he had ever talked to about everything and that telling a regular person made him take the next step. Inappropriate probably, but I laughed. He looked at me strangely and I said, "I can't remember ever being called a regular person." He laughed too and said, "I guess that's true, isn't it?" I just said, "Yeah. Thanks."

Back to serious, I asked what he meant. He told me that he had been back and forth with himself a lot, probably because he was a chicken, but he finally made the call. When I asked him what call, he smiled, "I'm going to get my head shrunk." I told him that was awesome, and he let me know that it wasn't as brave as it sounded. He told the department that he had to help with his daughter's team for the next few weeks on Tuesday afternoons and told his wife that he had to take this class if he ever wanted to think about making lieutenant. He added, "I'm also going out of town to do it. I'm not ready for anyone else to know about it. I have to see how I do with it first." He went on to tell me that's why he asked to meet then, because he wouldn't be able to do our scheduled time the next day. I congratulated him, and he just whispered out, "I guess we'll see." We bantered back and forth for a few minutes and set up a time for Thursday. As he was pulling away, he said, "Thank you for everything," and drove away before I could answer.

***

He was leaning against the side of his car as I walked up. The first thing out of his mouth was, "Well, that was interesting." I smiled and told him I bet it was. He then went on to tell me some of what had gone on and also said he was surprised. I asked him why and he said, "I think I've been watching too many movies. I thought I'd be lying on a couch and some guy with a funny accent would be nodding while writing notes and every once in a while, he'd say, 'I see.'" I laughed out loud and told him he needed to get out of his recliner and chase more criminals or something. He laughed and said, "Funny you should say that." I just looked at him. "I think I'm going to put in for a lateral move. A guy is being promoted and his spot is going to be open at the beginning of November." I asked him if he got all that from one session and he said it was a little of this and a little of that. He had already been thinking about it as a way to help himself and that when he went Tuesday and realized it wasn't every stereotype he had ever dreamed up that he thought that he should be engaged in the process too and that being proactive was a good start. I told him that he was right and that I had never heard him string together that many thoughts at once. He laughed and grew serious. "I don't know. I just feel like everything that's happening right now is the right thing. I know what I mean."

I asked him what his thoughts were on all these giant steps he was starting and what he hoped to gain from his self-reflection. He told me that although it sounded corny, he meant it. He wanted to be a better husband, father, and cop. In that order. I shared that if he was willing to do the work and follow through that all those things could happen. I ended the thought by saying, "But it's not going to be easy."

We spent quite a bit of time talking about everything going on. He looked tired, but, I guess, excited too. He looked motivated. I asked if he thought at some point, he would talk to his wife about all of it. He said, "I'm a big chicken right now. She's not just my wife, she's also my best friend." He went on to add, "In theory, I know she'd be there, but in reality, I have been lying to her for twelve years. If you really care, that's not what you do. I have to learn to truly accept what I've done. I think when I get to that place, I'll be ready to really hear her. I think it's going to be terrible. But, yes, eventually I have to tell her."

We talked for many minutes about what he'd done. I told him that I personally had very strong views on monogamy, commitment, and what vows meant but, that in this case, I would have to contradict myself somewhat as I told him not to rush until he was really ready. That if he pushed out of some sense of guilt or remorse it would definitely be the terrible he was envisioning. He just nodded.

To lighten things a little, I asked if he'd had any more ridiculous criminal adventures since we'd last spoken. He laughed, and we talked for about twenty minutes about the various mundanities and serious incidents that had gone on. It was a nice way to wrap up everything. I'd had a feeling before I went to meet him that this would probably be our last interview so I let him off the hook. As we finished, I reached and shook his hand and thanked him for being so open with me. Demonstrative for him, he hugged my shoulder, patted my back, then got back in the car and drove off. I stood in the alley and watched him go then turned and headed to the bus stop.

My Thoughts and Views

I had to think about him for a day or two before I could write it all down. He made it harder, because although he would be very easy to dislike, he is, in general, a nice guy.

Unfortunately, much of what he has done, I am unable to condone or accept. To use a position of power or authority to subjugate another can never be corrected. He can atone for his role in it, but, in reality, there is a ripple effect to his actions and there are so many ways that those involved were affected in the long run.

I do respect his honesty with me. I also respect his decisions now to do the right thing. Everyone has a point of self-realization in their life and you can't judge one's time by another's. This seems to be his time.

As he and I talked about, if he's willing to do the work and then follow it through, he can be what he told me. A good husband, a good father, and a good cop. I see his determination and it gives me hope. I think he'll make it.

The Sit Down Guy

Coastal Georgia. We met on the 10 early on a Saturday morning. It is a long route and takes an hour end-to-end. We had the bus to ourselves and plenty of time to talk. He was going to an outdoor event and his wife was meeting him later. He thought there was no point in driving two cars.

***

He defines himself as a good husband and father. When he was younger, a good son. A good co-worker, a good friend. An all-around good guy. Nice. People in his adult life most likely see exactly that since he's worked his entire life to be that way.

Born into an outwardly good family, they were wealthy and successful and had all the trappings that went with that life station. Whereas his twin sister was always the bad one, he was always the good. He was also a mama's boy.

As little kids, he and his sister were close in the brother/sister way. They played together and all that. But he didn't like her. He truthfully didn't understand her. That was the beginning of his childhood focus of self-preservation. He learned to be a changeling at a young age and to be the person that was amiable, easy to get along with, and nice.

From day one, his sister questioned everything. Every single thing. She said what she thought, mostly did what she wanted, she was very smart and also independent. From very early on, she got beat. Often.

He remembers, when they were little, watching it happen and then turning and hiding in their room. They shared one then. He would think to himself that if she'd just be good that wouldn't happen. He never even considered trying to stop it. If he did, then he'd be a bad one too, wouldn't he? His mother loved him the most. That's what he saw. He was also rewarded with anything he wanted. Just for being good. He liked nice things and over time he learned to shut up, not hear, and not see.

His growing years are completely intertwined with those of his twin. Somewhere inside, he loved her and respected her. He watched her continue to be herself as she got beat, beat more, and then beat again. She never changed. He hated her too.

He worked hard to assimilate, fit in, and to get along with everyone. Always. Inside, he often felt cowardly. But his mother loved him best.

His sister had to be so smart, so obnoxious. He didn't understand her. At all. He was sure she made him feel dumb on purpose as he watched her skip grades and move further away from him. He was embarrassed, saddened, probably jealous and angry too. He didn't like her though. In fact, he resented being connected to her by birth. She told him he was a pussy and a chicken and that he was just like their mother. He was her favorite.

As his sister joined boys' sports teams, usually his, the worlds collided. He was always the good sport, the team player. She marched in and kicked ass. He never wanted to stand out. She did without even trying to. He didn't want to admit he even knew her. He just wanted to fit in. He was still mom's favorite.

He ended up in the hospital at twelve. He had severe bleeding ulcers. From internalizing his life. He was in the hospital for a week. His mother was by his side. Junior High was a tough place. For him. Not for her. They went to the same school and she was two years ahead by then. He felt even more embarrassed and mad. He also couldn't pretend they weren't twins and now even more people knew he was dumb. He even got beat up by a classmate's brother on the bus one day.

His entire childhood was a reaction. To what people thought, what they did, how they dressed, and what they believed. Original thought was not in his lexicon. It wasn't safe. He had been watching silently since they were little as his sister continued to get beat by their father. Didn't she know if she just went along that wouldn't happen? Why couldn't she just be good like he was?

Not only did she not respect him, but his father didn't either. But he didn't hit him. Somewhere deep inside he knew it was because he didn't care enough to. He understood that was twisted but also the truth.

Their intertwined lives continued. As she skipped more grades and moved even further ahead of him, he was allowed to change schools so that big disparity wouldn't be the first thing everybody else saw. He didn't want everybody to think he was dumb.

When they were fifteen, he got the best present ever. He was so happy when his sister, with no comment or anything else, just left one day. Wasn't he? He had internalized any deep thought or feeling his entire childhood. It was safer to be judgmental, to learn to be the good one, and to stay invisible. He was a survivor of child abuse. Hers.

He blossomed some after she left and began to learn to be his own person. Going to a different school had been the right thing to do. He gained some popularity, which was new to him, though he tried to not stand out. Being a good-looking guy, the girls started to notice too. Although he'd always talked to everyone, that was different. By the end of that first year alone, he had a girlfriend. His mother loved her.

Through school, his athletic skills were honed, and he was offered a scholarship, even with his below-average grades, to a smaller college. His mother was so proud. Then about a week after he graduated high school, she was dead. And he was lost. His sister was gone, his father didn't like him, and the one he always looked to was no longer. He had no idea what to do. He had never had to think for himself. Or wanted to.

His girlfriend stepped up then and helped try to guide him into early adulthood as she got him off to college. Didn't work out though. The classes were too hard, and he no longer had his anchor. He dropped out before his first year was done.

He fell into, well, he doesn't know how to explain it. Maybe apathy? He cared about not much. He was acting like a jerk and a child. He was irresponsible and selfish. He didn't know how to find his own balance because he had never had to. It got so bad that his girlfriend ended up dumping him for six months with the parting shot that he really needed to grow up and get it together.

He worked at it some, his father even stepped in and got him a good job, but it didn't last. Nothing he did in his early twenties stuck. He was floundering. He thought of his sister at times. He had never seen or heard from her again. He had heard a few whispers a couple years back but that was it. He wondered, only sometimes, how she was. He thought of his mother too, often. But his girlfriend was right. He needed to grow up. He contacted her to get together and talk. He told her that he wanted to join the Army. She thought that was smart. They got back together soon after.

After basic training, he asked her to marry him. She said yes. After his school and before Germany, they got married and she went with him to his duty station. They started building a life. He sometimes thought he was playing at being a grownup, but his wife took their lives firmly in hand and directed him on what to do, etc. He was a happy man. From a childhood of the same, he felt safe and loved.

As they got settled in, his wife talked to him about contacting his sister. Since he had mostly zero family, she thought it was the right thing to do. She eventually convinced him. He had gone to school with her good friend from childhood. Since he had no idea where or if his sister was, his wife worked to find the friend's address. He wrote her a quick note and asked for any information she might have and a couple of weeks later got one back from her.

He didn't know why he was surprised, since she had always done whatever she wanted, but the friend told him that she was a chef. If he wanted to be honest, he knew she could cook, they all could, because his mother wasn't a very good one. The friend also told him that she lived with her girlfriend. He shook his head at that too. He knew she was gay; she had never hidden that either, it was just another way she was different, but he guessed he didn't think about her being, you know, gay in life. The friend also gave him the phone number she had.

Now it was up to him. It took him a little while to get up his nerve. He thought to himself, what would they talk about? It had been ten years since she had walked out the door. Once again, his wife stepped in and told him just to call and say hello and not worry about the rest. It took two calls to do it. The first time some woman answered and said she was out of town and wouldn't be back for a few days. The second time, she was there. He managed to stumble through a conversation with her, but he doesn't remember anything that was said. After that, he did the right thing and would try to call every once in a while, to keep the connection. She wasn't mean or anything, but he got the feeling that she didn't really care if he did or not. It was weird, but he felt like she had always been disappointed in him and there was nothing he could ever say to make it right. When he talked to his wife about how things were, she would just tell him that he had done what he thought was right at the time. He didn't think she agreed with his choices either.

Not long after, he found out he was going to be a father. He was excited, and surprised that he was in some ways. They were excited together. It was a really nice time in their lives as they worked to get ready for it. Her parents would be coming to Germany to spend time with them when the baby was born. He liked them, they were nice enough, but they were also very different from the way he was raised. He told his sister that she was going to be an aunt in one of their phone calls. She congratulated him but didn't seem to care otherwise.

He spent a lot of time that his wife didn't know about thinking about what kind of parent he would be. He'd had bad examples. His father had been like a mythic figure to him. He was a tyrant to his sister. He knew he would never be like that. For the first time, he admitted that his mother had been wrong too. He'd never had to or wanted to look at that. Not only had he often done the wrong thing, he was a little kid, but his mother had never done anything about what was happening either. He wasn't a deep thinker and the more he analyzed, the more he kept it to himself. But he knew he didn't want to be that kind of parent either. One of the thoughts that did come out was that he wondered if he should apologize to his sister. He pushed it back though. She probably wouldn't accept it. Still finding the easy route, he was actually keeping himself safe instead of putting himself out there.

Then the baby was born. He had a daughter. She was beautiful. He loved her from the start. He thought about his sister more then and wondered how his father could hurt a little girl and how strong his sister had been. He didn't tell anybody; he just knew he could and would never do that. He was going to be her protector and defender. She was definitely going to be daddy's girl.

That first month, while his wife's parents were there, he made a video for his father. He had shown even less excitement than his sister, but he wanted to share his happiness, and everyone wanted to be a grandparent, didn't they? He found out the answer was no. His father sent the video back and said he didn't have time to watch it. Again, he shouldn't have been surprised, but he was. His father really wasn't a nice person and just from what he could tell, he was worse now.

Being the head of a family changed him some. He had responsibilities not only to his wife, but now his daughter. It was time to man up some to make sure they would always be taken care of. He worked hard to do just that.

A year later, they found out another was going to join them. Nine months later, they had a son. He loved him from the start too but realized thoughts on sons and daughters were different. He found that interesting. By then, his time in the service was coming to an end or to reenlistment. It had been a great bridge but was not a career for him. They were going home and would live near her family while they got settled and decided what their next steps would be. Once again, his wife stepped in and suggested stopping and seeing his sister on the way. They ended up spending a long weekend with her and her girlfriend, though they had put them in a hotel. His daughter was two, his son was only nine days old. That was the last time he ever saw her.

Their father died about a year later and he called his sister to tell her the news. He was upset, and she thought that was ridiculous. When he asked her if she was coming home for the funeral, she actually laughed. What did he expect? He still remembered exactly what she said to him that day. She'd said, "You know, at some point in your life you're going to have to stand up for something, if for no other reason than to keep from getting run over." That was the last time he ever spoke to her.

***

It's now been twenty-six years since that conversation. He is a different person as an adult, but his personality is much the same. He still works to be the good one, the nice one, and the easy to get along with. From a life of internalizing most everything, he still has gastric issues.

He is still married to the same beautiful girl and they have three children, all young adults now. It is in his role of parent that he is most proud. He has great kids. All are most definitely their own people, and all are doing well.

He looks at his youngest daughter and, even now, sees his sister. She is so much like her that it's spooky. She too, has always done her own thing in her own way. She has also always had that inner-confidence and is scared of nothing. And, she is also gay. Which, oddly, he never considered. But she even looks like her. No deep thinker still, it seems like the circle of life.

Although he never talked to his sister again and doesn't know if she's dead or alive, he still thinks about her now and then. Never shared in depth, she has become a magical figure to his kids. When they were little, he was still angry and confused and really didn't talk about her at all. But, through the years since he has shared a few stories he remembers. But he knows, that in reality, they were strangers as children and they still are. He guesses they always will be.

My Thoughts and Views

Although I haven't shared every experience, nor included everything we talked about, I have shown the continuity of his life in his want to always be safe and well-liked.

Overall, he's not a bad sort. I guess, looking at it, he's like a lot of people in the world. He wants to have his small place in it, he doesn't look at the big picture often, if at all, and he is firmly one of the masses and likes being there.

On the flip side, he is a coward. He has spent his life in the shallow end of the pool, too afraid to dive in anywhere deep. Although, in general, he is a good guy, as I listened to him backpedal and make reasons and excuses for always taking the easy way out, I have no respect for him.

The Jolly Rancher

SW Florida. We met at the bus stop waiting for the 7S to take us downtown. He was rolling his suitcase behind him. We both were headed to the same place, the library. We continued talking as we walked and continued it further when we got there.

***

He is twenty-seven and alternative in most every way: lifestyle, music, way of dress, and personal beliefs. He is a vegan that grew up on a cattle ranch in central/western South Dakota, not far from the banks of the Missouri river. The biggest city was nowhere close, about two-hundred-and-fifty miles in a couple of different directions.

The town he's from has about three-hundred families, or about one-thousand people. The entire county has just over two-thousand. Most everybody is white, dresses the same, votes the same, believes the same, and does the same. He told me he believes he's one of the very few that were different, and he personally only knew of one other.

When we first started talking, I told him that was one of the two states I hadn't been to. He said, "You're not missing anything." Then he added, "Unless you're a tourist. There's some cool stuff to see. For about a week. But then what? You go back home. For me, it was home." I said that there had to be something he liked, and he answered, "The same thing I hated the most. Wide open spaces."

In his small hometown he was considered "the weird one." "You know, we only had two black families. Two. This is

2018 and the fact that I knew that and knew them all, I shake my head. I don't think the people in my town could even spell diversity." We talked about growing up surrounded by whiteness and had similar thoughts on that. He continued, "I mean, I am white. But, damn, you know?" I understood what he meant and told him although older and from the south, I often felt that way growing up. He just nodded and said, "Right?"

We talked about his family. He's right in the middle, the problem child, with an older sister and younger brother. "Bossy and bratty," he added. I asked about his parents. "I have mixed thoughts, I'm sure they'll change as I get older, but my dad is harsh, I mean he runs a ranch, and my mom is a housewife. She does volunteer crap too though." I laughed at that one and he smiled.

I asked about pets and he nodded. "A bunch. With the ranch, we had everything plus some just showed up and stayed. We always had so many. I couldn't even tell you how many that was."

I asked him to tell me about his hometown a little more. "I think the town is less than three square miles, I know it is. I really did know everybody. It's a shame, that small and we would actually 'go into town.' Most had farms or ranches, so they were just outside the town limits and a lot of the others worked either at the co-op or the biodiesel place. The rest just had regular jobs. You know." I asked what he did. He said that when he was young that his dad was raising him to work the ranch. "I used to cry. Seriously. All the time. I hated it. I think he tried everything he could to 'make a man out of me.' But I really couldn't stand it. It was awful. That's when they all first started thinking something was wrong with me."

He continued, "I wouldn't eat meat. I mean, I saw them alive and happy, and they killed them for what? So I could have a cheeseburger? I heard things like: This is what's keeping a roof over your head, taking care of you, and letting you be a brat. That's also when I started getting called a faggot a lot."

I asked him if he was gay. He shook his head and said, "No. That was just the worst word they could think up, I guess." I asked about school and he shrugged. "I went. I graduated. All that. But it was surreal sometimes. Everybody played football, listened to country music, and drove trucks. I was in band, listened to alternative, punk, and rock, and I had a beat-up old Toyota. Faggot came up a lot then too." I asked if he had any friends. "Not really. I mean, I talked to people, knew them all, but mostly hung around one girl. She was like goth or whatever. Wore black, had dramatic makeup, scowled a lot." He made that face and I laughed out loud. He said, "It is funny, but is was us against everybody else. She left before I did. California, I think."

I asked if she was his girlfriend. "Definitely not. I had a couple of girls come around but never actually dated anybody. I doubt they told anybody they did anyway. I never said anything. That's for sure. It would have given my parents hope if they thought that maybe I really was 'normal.'" We both laughed.

I asked him where or if he worked. He said that he liked to cook and there was this kind of roadhouse slash bar slash restaurant slash meeting place and he cooked there from eleventh grade on.

***

At our second meeting, we picked up where we left off as I asked him what he'd been doing since he got here. Then I switched mid-thought and asked him why he picked here. He told me he had grown up never seeing an ocean. He added, "This is my first one. It's crazy." He went on to tell me the river was really nice, but. We sidetracked again, and I got him talking about something good from there. He said that one thing was kind of cool. That, as a crow flew, he was only about twenty-five miles from the southeastern end of a huge Indian reservation and that he had managed to get across the river and into it a few times. "But, if you want to go in front, it's about a hundred and fifty miles. You have to go up and around."

We worked our way back to here and he said he knew he wanted ocean and warm. He had already decided against the west coast. "Too expensive and I may be considered weird at home but there I think I'd just be a country boy in the big city." I laughed, and he told me that left the southeast. He looked at the Georgia coast and liked a lot about it but thought even that would be too cold. He'd had enough of that to last a lifetime. So, that left Florida. He didn't like the east coast for the same reasons he hadn't liked California, so he focused on the west. When he started researching here, he liked the music, the art, and a lot of other things he found so in the end, he picked here.

I then went back to what he was doing now. "I've only been here two months. I think I've ridden every bus everywhere, learning where things are." He told me once he was comfortable, he started applying for jobs and that he wanted to get in a hotel or better restaurant so he could learn more about the field because he really enjoyed it. "I have two in now that I really think I have a shot at. I guess I'll see." I told him it was about snowbird time and I was sure he would. He smiled.

I asked him about staying at the shelter. He said it was the cheapest thing while he was getting settled, that it wasn't like people thought, that is was more like a big dorm for people that were starting over. He didn't mind most of the street people he'd met. "It sounds funny, but I know what I mean. At least they're real, you know? Another thing for me though, is that it's almost sad to see so many homeless people. We had zero. Not one." He continued, "We had a couple of town drunks, but everybody knew where everybody lived, and someone would just take them home. I guess that doesn't happen in bigger places." I told him that by neighborhood it probably still did some but then I pointed out that technically he was homeless. He nodded. "I know. Yeah. I'm comfortable with that word right now. But, that's not what I meant." I told him that I actually understood what he meant but was pointing that out to show him he was grouping people like some would group him. He just nodded and said, "Yeah."

I asked him about finding a place and he said he had been looking at rooms or roommates on Craigslist when he went to the library. He said he had seen a few that would be good, but he didn't want to jump without a job. He said as soon as someone said yes, he would find a place. I asked him if he thought of school or anything like that. He said if he did anything it would be culinary school since that was what he wanted to do. That made sense to me.

***

We ended up meeting a week later than we were supposed to because he told me that he had some things to take care of. When I walked downtown to meet him, I found him sitting on a bench in the park beside the library with his rolling suitcase beside him. He looked up and smiled as I sat down.

We spent a few minutes just chatting about this and that and then I asked him what he had been up to. He told me that both of the places he'd told me about had contacted him for interviews. I nodded and said, "I told you they would. That's awesome. And?" "Well, the hotel, I went back for a second interview. The Chef there is cool. I met with the Sous Chef at the first one, then him at the second. After he understood that I wasn't just looking for a job but a career, he explained how the culinary world worked when you were working your way up and through. He said that hotels were a great place for that because they had large kitchens, did a lot of different things, and actually had a structured way that the kitchen worked. I'm not sure if he talks to everybody like he talked to me or if he took a special interest, but it was pretty great." I told him that it was probably some of both and that he was right about hotels, they were a great place to learn anything you wanted to. I also added that if he did find a chef that truly realized his potential that he should jump on that because he could stay with him for as long as he chose and truly learn the business like he wanted to.

He asked me how I knew so much about it and I laughed. I explained that in my first life I had been an Executive Chef for seventeen years. He smiled huge. "I had no idea." I laughed and told him I had never wanted to be anything else but that this was about him, not me. "Okay. I get it. That's cool though." I told him it most definitely was but then got him back on track and asked, "So?" "Well. So. I'm going to say yes. He wanted my answer by today. He didn't want me to jump, he wanted me to understand what it involved and to fully commit myself to the process. He gave me this printout of kitchen structure, how you moved up and through it, and some basic job descriptions. He told me that he would want me to start out in prep." I explained why and how much he would learn that way. "Yeah. I know I don't look it, but I'm really excited. This is a great opportunity and it's a higher end national chain too. If I do well, this could be a lifetime thing." I told him that it most definitely could, but he'd better focus on learning to cut vegetables without cutting his finger off first. He started laughing and said, "Right?"

We talked about his housing situation and he told me now that he knew where he was going to be, he had a better idea of where he wanted to live. That made sense to me. He added that after we talked, he was going in the library to visit his buddy, Craigslist, and I laughed.

I told him I was really interested to hear how it all shook out and that I would like to meet with him another time before he got started. He said, "Oh, definitely." When we were done with the interview, we sat for another forty-five minutes as I told him stories and experiences of the culinary world and the type things he could expect to happen. It was very nice to share that part of my life and he seemed to enjoy it as well.

***

For our last interview, I got there first. I was hanging in front of the library when he came walking up with a big smile on his face. Before he sat down, he said, "I am now gainfully employed." I told him that was terrific, and he agreed, still smiling big.

He sat down then, and we talked about that a little more, then I asked him if he had been in contact with his family at all. He shook his head and said, "I know it's kind of immature, I get that, but I guess I'm kind of mad at them right now." I told him that admitting how he felt was good, just not to let it become a lifetime thing. We talked for a few about some familial experiences I had gone through and how I came to an understanding. He sat and nodded as he said, "That's pretty cool. I'm working on it though. I don't hate them or anything that stupid, I'm just trying to understand why my difference scared them so much. They were really mean at times. All because of that." I told him that he just said why. That they were scared. Often people will see that difference and question themselves. That scares them. In a place like where he grew up, that sameness is a safety net and when somebody bucks the system it's looked at as a type of betrayal, like their choices weren't the right ones. I explained that was obviously a broad generalization but from a lifetime of talking to and listening to people that the thing I saw most often when I saw anger like that was fear. "I agree with you. My thoughts haven't gotten quite that developed yet, but that's really true, isn't it?" I told him that, yes, it was often that in one form or another. Some worked through it and got over it and some never did. He added, "My dad is so stubborn. I told you he was harsh. He might be one of the ones that never does." I told him when he was ready that he had to at least throw it out there and see if it came back. That he could only do what he could do. He nodded again, "Right?"

We moved onto his housing situation then. He said Craigslist was his guiding light, then laughed. He went on to tell me that he again found two, his new lucky number, and in the next couple of days would be talking to both. He went on to say that first with email, then by phone, they had all seemed all right. He had one of each to talk to. One was a roommate situation with two other guys his age and the other was renting a room from a lady that seemed nice too. I told him that I guessed it depended on whether he wanted a quiet place to rest or a bit of a party atmosphere. He agreed and said if all was cool with the lady, he would most likely choose that.

We sat and talked for a while then went our separate ways.

My Thoughts and Views

He'd probably roll his eyes, but I see him as a good kid. He's actually a nice guy. He is also a deep thinker. With so much alone time and with the difference he always had, he has had a lot of time to think things through from many different directions. That has helped him gain a balanced perspective about who he is, what he wants, and what he is comfortable with. As he settles and grows more, I can visualize that perspective applying to anything he chooses to engage in. He grew up as a fish out of water. Now he has found his place. I think he'll swim along just fine.

<u>The Care Less Girl</u>

West Texas. We met at the main bus station in El Paso. She sat down next to me and smiled so I struck up a conversation. A good first impression as I found her intelligent, funny, and friendly. We hopped on a bus together and continued our conversation. During that, I noticed that she is somewhat detached from what others think or feel. She doesn't really care.

She grew up in what would be considered a good or normal family. Mother, father, brother, dogs, cats. Very nice home. Very nice neighborhood. Summer home. Upper end of upper middle class. White. Socially connected. And the world that comes with all that.

From what she tells me, she was suffocating in the whiteness of her world. She understood she was different from a very early age and told me that although she could easily be and often was the black sheep, she saw herself more as multi-colored. Her family didn't get her, and she didn't get them. That never changed.

Although we talked mostly light on our bus trip, she agreed to meet me the next day at the library. She walked in with a smile on her face and as she sat down shared some early pictures of herself with me. I had to laugh; not just at her description of her thoughts at the time, but at the pictures. I didn't know her but her face showed what she was telling me. I think she was probably a smart ass from the start. As we've talked, she's shared some events from her early years and I shake my head.

I spoke to her for four days and got to see a lot of different sides of her personality so I can visualize those same traits on a young person. She told me that when she went out into the big world – school activities, athletics, etc., that it was obvious to her that not only did her family not get her, but most others didn't either. She wondered if it was her.

Although she didn't really care, and it didn't bother her; it did make her analyze not only herself but the world in general. Her intellect is also on the high side and combined with her personality as it is now, I can also visualize the reactions of others to her. Just watching how they do now have been interesting for me. I think for the most part she doesn't notice. Or care about that either.

She said as she got a little older, she was bored. Bored with her white world, bored with school, bored with many of the people around her, just bored. She also was (and still is) a loner. She spent a lot of her early years alone. During that alone time, she pondered all the questions she had about herself and about others and about the world. About everything.

The boredom, the thoughts, the intellect, and the personality are what led her to the black sheep part of her life.

***

She told me the first drink of liquor she took was somewhere around the end of fourth grade. She added that the first joint she smoked and the first cigarette was then as well. So was her first real sexual experimentation. I asked her if something had happened at that time. She told me that she had thought about that for a long time but couldn't remember any big thing. She said it was more when she first began to realize that she had (emotionally) absent parents and also when she began to notice that people outside of her family cared about things that just didn't seem to matter. Since on some scale she had always done her own thing, her parents didn't seem to notice nor care when she started moving to the other side. They were busy. So was the world.

I asked if she did all those things to get drunk, high, or get some kind of reaction. She told me that, being honest, there was probably some of that, but it was more to get a reaction from herself. She knew even then that she really didn't care what other people thought and by that age had started to wonder if something was wrong with her. She was nine.

As we talked about that time and place more, she told me that when those types of thoughts first started that she wrote in what is now called a journal but was then called a diary. She kept it hidden in her room. She told me that she had always written in it, but her mother found it read it and then shared her disappointment. She laughed and shook her head when she used that word. I asked if disappointment was a euphemism for what really occurred, and she told me that yes, it was.

She told me that her world was two sides growing up. Outwardly, she was a good student, she did all the usual activities – scouts, sports, sleepovers; but inwardly she just really didn't care. She tried to convey that she understood that sounded odd or cold. She told me that it didn't mean that she didn't enjoy them and have fun, but that in the long run, she just wasn't particularly connected to them, the people, or the outcome. That saddened me some as I could see the young girl she was just watching the world go on around her.

As we moved forward through her school years, they went
by most rapidly and were much the same as the early ones.
She said that as she got older that her level of detachment
grew, her personality got stronger, and the reactions of
many other people became more noticeable.

***

The first time she cut herself she was fourteen. She talked
about it like it was nothing really. No emotion attached. I
don't know if that was for my benefit or not, but it still
made me sad. I've sidetracked. She told me she had really
started focusing on the lack of care and often the lack of
emotion that went with. She told me that when she cut
herself, she felt something. And it felt good. That first time
she used a broken drink bottle that she had found when she
was walking in the woods. Alone. Although she ended up
getting tetanus from that first experience, she admitted that
she had finally found something that made her feel. Pain.

***

At the beginning of our next conversation, I steered a little
back toward her family. As with most things, she was
succinct in her descriptions. I asked her if she could pick
who she was the most like and she joked that she must have
been adopted, then laughed. I noticed that she usually joked
when she didn't want to answer. This was no different.

So, through school she went, falling more on the dark side
of her choices and thoughts. By the time high school
arrived, she turned and walked away. She was tired of
being bored. She left school, she left home, she left her
family, she left her friends. She headed toward herself.

***

She just slowly shook her head when I started asking about what she did when she left home. She answered simply when she said, "Everything." I asked her how old she was, and she told me sixteen and added that it was a different time then. She also added that she had been surprised that her parents had an opinion when she left. They had seemed upset. She shook her head at that too.

As the story continued, we went back and forth a little when I asked about her substance use. She told me that from that first time it wasn't a bunch because she was just a young kid, but once she got to junior high it became, as she described, above average.

When she left, she moved in with a couple of friends and fell into what she describes as the world of sex, drugs, and rock 'n' roll. She told me stories of that time that still make my eyes raise and I'm in no way naive. But as usual, she seemed unfazed by anything that went on.

I asked about that period more in depth. She said that first step out lasted about six months. And laughed. When I asked her what was so funny, she told me that during that time she had done a little of any and everything and it ended when she OD'd while driving and crashed. I asked her if she got hurt. Her only comment was that yes, she had. She didn't want to talk about it anymore. I'm not sure how that part of her life ended or anything else about what happened, but it must have been bad because just as we started to move on, she told me that she had never touched any kind of alcohol or drug again. I'm assuming it was terrible. Same as I've repeated though; she seems detached from that too.

***

A few months later she joined the Army. She told me that
she actually enjoyed all the hardcore stuff in the beginning;
winning awards for different things, but when that was
done it was just a job in ugly clothes. She quickly became
bored. She enjoyed the travel and a lot of people she met
but she found it stupid that you had to follow orders just
because someone outranked you, since many of them were
idiots.

I will take an aside here and tell you that you will see that
as a theme throughout much of her life. Authority. Not her
work ethic, talent, skill, motivation, job performance, or
anything else; just her inability to listen to, as she says,
idiots just because they have a position above yours. She is
overall tolerant of others. I think it's mainly because she
doesn't care, but she deals badly with stupid. We talked a
little about jobs in connection with that and she said that if
you counted just part-time ones or side jobs, she'd had
about seventeen by her mid-twenties.

Back to the Army though. She made good rank. She got the
appropriate "I was there" medals as well as a couple for
other things. She did not get a good conduct medal. She
laughed again since that is mostly automatic. But not for
her. She told me she had managed to make it down to two
months left in before she finally shook the branch. I don't
know all the lingo, but she told me that her battalion
commander had been very nice and had gotten promoted to
Brigadier General and moved. For her last two months they
got an officer that was an idiot and an asshole. And she was
so close to done that she couldn't hide her thoughts. Not
that she had ever been good at that anyway. I guess not
very long before she got out, a couple of weeks I think, he
had called her into his office and asked her opinion of him

"off-the-record." She told him that he was an asshole. She said he proved her point though as he tried to make the little time she had left as miserable as possible. He was also responsible for her not getting the good conduct medal. She told me the day she got out, she walked out of the office where her paperwork was done, dropped her full duffel bag in the trash, and kept right on going.

***

As our next conversation began, we began talking about relationships she's had. She made a face when I questioned her. She tried to explain that she's had a few shorter term one and that she liked the women she was with, but overall, she both cared and didn't. When I asked her to expand that she told me that she mostly enjoyed them while they were happening, but that if they would have ended at any time, it wouldn't have bothered her.

I called her out a little bit since they had all ended and asked if she had ever been broken up with. She told me that she hadn't; it was always her that left. I tried to get more in depth and asked her if she had ever sustained a long-term relationship and she asked what I considered long term. I answered ten years. With no amplification she said, "Just one." I asked her then if she had ever truly loved or been in love with any of them. She also answered, "Just one." When I asked if it was the long term one, she just said "No." Then she changed the subject.

I tried to continue with relationships – parents, siblings, friends, neighbors. She told me that she genuinely liked many but was still mostly disconnected. She added that with any kind of inter-personal relationships that the things she was sharing with me were only seen or known by her. That it was extremely rare if anyone else ever noticed.

I continued pushing some and asked if she had knowingly ever used someone. Her only answer was, "Yes." Then she changed the subject again.

***

Back in self-analyzation mode, she told me that for quite a while she had studied split personalities because even though most probably didn't or couldn't see it, she distinctly could see two separate parts of herself. We talked about that for most of one afternoon. In some ways she seems to understand herself pretty well. Though she has no desire to change any of it, she does have a good degree of self-awareness.

We talked about that more and she said a lot stemmed from her old standard – boredom. In any pursuit she can be engaged, enjoy herself immensely, be present, committed, and the rest, but in the long run, she always walked away. She likes or loves the person or experience at the time but still fades away eventually. When asked, she said that no, it didn't sadden her, not really. But she had enough emotion to feel bad for a moment, particularly if it had been really good. She might not have been sad, but I was for her.

***

I flipped it the next day and asked her if she was ever angered. She admitted that every once in a while, she'd get that way, but it took a lot to get her there. She went on to add that it usually was just lack of sense, decency, brains, or whatever. Whether it be in speech or deed. She also doesn't care for people that try to dominate or bully others.

She added that in instances like that she always shared her thoughts. Otherwise her mouth was shut unless she was just having shallow conversation or unless someone asked her opinion.

***

During our last conversation I went back and asked her some follow up questions that I had jotted down about subjects we had left open. The first was about pain. I asked if that had continued to be a theme in her life and she told me that it was, but she had found other ways to channel it. She did not amplify. I asked if she considered it self-harm. She joked, not a surprise, that she didn't. She just considered it free electric-shock therapy. I let that subject go and asked her more about relationships and if she'd reconnected with any of the people we had talked about. She answered, "Just one." When I asked which she changed the subject again. I asked if she had reconnected with any family and she told me that she had not. I did get to laugh a little with her when I asked about career. She smiled when she said that she had found years ago that she did much better when she worked for herself and ended up doing that most of her adult life.

My Thoughts and Views

She was personable and intelligent. As far as her look at split-personality; she is definitely not. I think because she spends a lot of time alone, she just sees what's inside of her and what's outside of her more than others might. I studied some of the various disorders and you really can't peg her. She does have some of the anti-social tendencies – the lack of care with what others think or see and lack of emotion. But she also seems to have many of the borderline parameters – the lack of care overall, self-harm, boredom, and other traits along those lines.

She is comfortable with who she is. She called herself a rover and she definitely is that, but she is also a loner. She is comfortable in that aloneness even when she is with or around others.

<u>The American</u>

North Carolina. We met riding the 4 on a Sunday morning on the way to a great flea market. I was going to shop and he was going to meet his wife who had gone earlier to get a good spot.

***

Although we'd talked a little on the bus two days before, our first meeting was at his jobsite during his lunch break.

As I walked up, he said, "Se habla espanol?" I laughed. "Perquito. Muy perquito, amigo." He smiled and said, "Well, I guess we'll have to work on that."

We were sitting in the opening of what would be sliding-glass doors. We were about eight floors up, swinging our feet in the open air. I even got to wear a hard hat. It was at the construction site where he was working. Another damn hotel to me. Job security to him. Different perspectives. We smiled and began to get to know each other.

He grew up in the Mexican state of Sonora. It's a big one. Known for its very nice beaches on the west coast and it's drug-running and border crossing to the north, it is actually a very diverse state in every way. But, as he says, his family lived in the poorer part, and he emphasizes that most are poor, near the desert region. He said between the drug lords, the corrupt government officials, and the mostly corrupt federales' that life was often stressful since you never knew who the good guys were or if there were any. His mother is simple but kind, and he has eight brothers and sisters. He is the oldest. His father died when he was sixteen and it was his job to take care of his family. He headed west to Baja California just after he turned seventeen and crossed into the United States to do just that.

He met some others during and just after the crossover and got a job picking lettuce in California. It was hard work, very hard, but he felt a sense of community and of purpose. And he was free. That meant everything.

He often worried about his family. As mentioned, they weren't in the best area. It wasn't the worst either, but still he worried. As he told me, it wasn't like the pretty postcards most see. He told me that not only did many Americans not understand his culture, but they didn't understand the way Mexican society worked when it came to family. He said that from what he had seen over the years, young people here move out, get a job, an apartment and start making a life. His experience was different. He had responsibilities to make sure they were all okay. He picked lettuce for about a year and a half.

Once he was more comfortable with English and with getting around, he went with a friend to Los Angeles. He immediately got two jobs – one in a restaurant and another cleaning office buildings late at night. He moved into a two-bedroom apartment with seven others. There were two sets of bunk beds in each bedroom. He began working seventy-five to eighty hours a week. He was eighteen then.

He sent two thirds of the money to his mother and lived off the other third. He joked that he and the woman at Western Union became friends, he was there so much. He had started off sending international money orders but that was a pain so on Western Union day his mother and one of his brothers would ride three buses to the town that had an office and then ride three home. He was tired but proud that he was able to take care of his family.

***

He is a handsome guy now. He laughed to cover his embarrassment when I told him that and told me that his sisters were beautiful. He pulled out his phone and began showing me pictures of his family. He looked just like his mom and he said they had the same personality too. He was a mama's boy. As he scrolled through, he showed me an older one of him taken not long after he crossed over. I told him he looked like a baby. He said that really, he was, barely seventeen.

***

We went back to him and I asked him what it felt like to come here. His eyes actually watered a little and he quietly said, "It felt like freedom." He went on to tell me that for people that have always had it and take it for granted that it will always be there, that it was hard to explain. He said to be in a place where you had the opportunity to be exactly what you wanted to be every single day was mostly overwhelming to him. He added that, yes, you had to work hard for it, but it was there. Just waiting. He shook his head and smiled.

***

Still illegal, after about five years in Los Angeles, he moved east to North Carolina. He liked LA some, but it was crowded and expensive. He had a cousin in North Carolina and a job already waiting for him. The pay was about the same, but it was much less expensive to live there.

He got settled into an apartment much like the one he had left. Once he did that, he got a second job again. And for the first time since he had left Mexico, he got to play organized soccer. That was his happy place. I asked him how he had time to do all that and he said when it was important you made time. I agreed.

He ended up staying in North Carolina. One skill that he'd had that became more developed was that he was good with his hands. Although he worked part time in a restaurant at night, he became a full-time construction worker and as he told me, learned more, worked harder, and really enjoyed himself.

He was enticed to stay with his company by his boss. They thought well of him and wanted to help him to continue his work and development in the construction field. With the extra attention and training, he would be able to work as much as he wanted. He liked the company, his boss, and what he was doing. He was a very happy man.

***

As far as his family in Mexico at the time, now that some of his other siblings were older, much of the pressure was off him. For the first time since he'd come to the US, he had some time to focus on himself. He had always been around open markets and flea markets in Mexico and he began spending his weekends at bargain places, yard sales, and flea markets. When he had enough stocked up, he continued to shop on Saturdays and began selling where I met him on Sundays.

During all this time of growth he was happy but missed his family. Because he was in the US illegally, he could not go home. They talked and facetimed all the time, but it wasn't the same. It bothered him a lot.

***

He loved America so much, but he loved something else too. A woman that he met not long after moving to North Carolina. She was a seller then as well and they met while both were selling their wares at the flea market where we were both headed when I met him.

As their relationship grew and things got more serious, they often talked about their future together. But he was still illegal, and he wanted everything to be right, so they began doing a lot of research to see what needed to be done to make him legal. Then they had to find the right lawyer to handle it. His boss and company helped them find just the right immigration attorney. Once that was set, then they had to have the money to do it all. That stage took about a year.

What had to be done after all the paperwork was completed was that he had to go back to Mexico and come back through the US Embassy with his approved green card.

It was a very nerve-racking time and he told me that they were both worried and stressed, but excited too. The time moved fast, it felt too fast at times, then it was time to go. On a wing and a prayer, off he went with neither of them knowing what would happen.

He was gone for almost a month. He told me that he was both happy and scared. Happy that he would be able to start a family with the woman he had fallen in love with yet scared that something might happen, and he wouldn't be allowed to go.

He had to go to Mexico City to the embassy there and did not see his family during that time, though they talked daily. He and his girlfriend also talked constantly. He told me the waiting was the hard part. Some days, he would be excited, some days worried. Although confident, he was still nervous, so it was on pins and needles that he waited.

Then, like the miracle that it was to them, he was approved. He is a very macho guy, but he said he cried like a baby from happiness and relief. Of course, his comedic side also showed, and he went and bought a bunch of T-shirts, stickers, and other things with all kinds of immigrant nonsense on them. He thought that was funny and he still wears the ones he still has when he's in the mood.

As an aside, I asked him what he would have done had he not been approved. And he answered, "The same thing I did the first time."

When he made it home, the first thing he did was ask her to marry him. She said yes. Emotional again, he said his soon-to-be wife understood what he had gone through and how hard he had worked for so long, and that first Thanksgiving after he became legal, she gave him his Christmas present early. It was a roundtrip ticket to spend Christmas with his family. He had not seen them in almost fourteen years. He softly said, "That's love. Besides her saying yes, that was the best present I ever received."

***

At the beginning of our second meeting, we moved on to prejudice next. We both found it completely ridiculous in any way, shape or form. But Mexicans are the face of that hatred now. We talked for quite a while about his experiences and all the different things that had happened to him and then we both talked about all the various names we had been called and comments we had heard. He said, "If it wasn't turning so mean now, it would be funny. But we are all North Americans. Until people from Europe came here and started taking different areas for their countries then drawing lines on a map, we were all the same." I told him that was true, then he laughed. When I asked why, he said that years ago, for something they had to do in Mexico, he was too little to understand what it had been, most of the people he knew, including his family, had their blood taken. A few months later, a health official told his parents that their family was considered Native American by the state. He said he never really gave it a thought but now, with the way things are, he finds that particularly amusing.

***

I backtracked a little and asked him about that first Christmas with his family. His eyes teared again. He quietly said, "Unbelievable." He went on to say that although he saw them in videos, pictures, and facetime, that to see his entire family was crazy. His mom did it up. It was like the prodigal son returning from the wars. It was as much a family reunion as a holiday celebration. He met nieces and nephews that hadn't existed when he left as well as catching up with everyone else, and just spending time with them all. He went to Mass on Christmas day and he laughed when he said the family took up two rows. He was there for ten days and he said though it was the most amazing time, he missed his girlfriend a lot and they had also talked every day while he was there. Her Spanish wasn't great, and his family's English wasn't either, but she managed to meet most everyone on facetime.

***

Our third meeting was at a local park with a lot of things for kids to do that included a train that goes around it and a large pond with paddle boats. We continued where we had stopped the last time. They got married on Valentine's Day, a month and a half after he came back from Mexico. He smiles, looking back. That was five years ago. He told me that he was a lucky man in so many different ways.

Over these last five years, they have built a good life together and, as he says, he loves her even more now. I believe him. His face lights up whenever he talks about her. He still works construction, and she is still a seller. He still joins her on Sundays. They have been to Mexico together a few times as well.

He also now has a daughter of his own. She is three-and-a-half. Even though she is a good combination of him and his wife, she looks a lot like him and his mother. He smiles huge. "Daddy's girl." She's a cutie, that's for sure. I got to know her a little since she decided she wanted to sit on my lap most of the time we were talking. She acts just like him too. He laughed.

The three of us sat at the waterfront and played and chatted for about an hour, talking about serious and not. It was an enjoyable way to spend a weekend morning. I had to ride the train with them that day before I left. They both smiled the entire time.

***

For our last meeting, we were once again on the roof. He is now a foreman for his construction company and also helps oversee the work at three different job sites. His work ethic is committed, and he get things done, but he never forgets his humor while doing them. Being bilingual is also a huge asset and he communicates comfortably with everyone. He is as loyal to his job as he is to his family. His boss is still the one that gave him a chance when he moved here, and he has stayed with him ever since. I met him too and he is a cool guy. I also said hello to quite a few of the men and women working. You can tell that they think just as well of him as he does of them.

As our time ended, I asked him to describe himself. He tried to be goofy, which isn't hard for him, and I told him to be serious. He thought about it for a minute. "I would say that I am blessed. In every way I can be. I was born and raised in a good family. I have had so many opportunities because of the good people I have met along the way. I have a beautiful wife and beautiful daughter. I have work that I love. I am a son, a husband and a father. I am a satisfied man."

My Thoughts and Views

For some reason, when I think of him, my mind goes back to medieval times. He is a cross between the court jester and a knight in shining armor. He rides his own path without ever losing his loyalty to and care for the people in his life. Within that though, he never loses his sense of humor. The word that always comes to me is honor. He is an honorable kind of guy. And I am honored too, as he shared his life with me.

<u>The Nonsensical One</u>

California. He and his crew were half asleep and half high as I walked down the sidewalk between Sunset Boulevard and Hollywood Boulevard. Of course they were taking up an entire bus stop for a bunch of routes by having their persons, their sleeping bags and their crap spread all over it. He asked me for a cigarette and I told him it would be a dollar or a story. A story it would be.

***

He describes himself as a street shaman, a philosopher. He says his life is romantic, exciting, adventurous. He is free to roam and do as he pleases. He is the definition of what freedom is supposed to mean. My opinion varies greatly from that description.

***

He was born to hippie parents in the flower power era of the late sixties and early seventies. He grew up in the Rainbow Family during its early years.

His grandmother left Wisconsin, moving to Hollywood. She hadn't been there long when she met a man. When she realized she was pregnant, they decided they should get married. Turns out that both quickly realized it hadn't been their best choice. Grandma also realized that she didn't really want a kid. She left soon after, leaving the new baby with her husband. His mother, as a toddler, was raised by her father and stepmother. They also decided they didn't really want the responsibility and she was turned over to an orphanage.

As she got a bit older, her abandonment issues became more pronounced, wondering why they had given her away. She ended up leaving the orphanage in her mid-teens and made her way to upstate New York in early 1969. She met a man they called Grandpa Woodstock, who had three sons of his own. He had also taken responsibility for nine girls much like her, and she became his tenth ward.

She eventually hooked up with one son, and they fell into the hippie world. They also eventually joined up with the beginnings of the Rainbow Family. They all took to the road, protesting Vietnam and whatever else caught their fancy at the time. He was born during this time in the back of a van outside Corpus Christi in 1972.

As with much of his actual life, this cannot be verified in any way, but I take that story with a grain of salt. You should too. I sat on the sidewalk by that same bus stop in Hollywood as he told that story. He doesn't look you in the eye when he tells it. He looks up and away, like he's refining it as he goes to fit who he's telling it to.

***

The three times I met with him, I watched. All the others around him are in their twenties. A couple roll their eyes when he talks. The rest drink it like it's mother's milk as he works to make being homeless and high romantic. It's really not. It's dirty, it's cold, it's harsh, it's dangerous, it's lonely, it's dispiriting. It's a bunch of other things as well.

One that he initially convinced is now his street wife. She says she's twenty-six. I'm not sure about that. He says he's forty-five and looks older than me. The day-to-day truth came out as I was getting bored listening to him and started asking her questions instead. She's only been on the street a little over a year so she's not hard. She's in shock of her world now. But she still mostly believes him. I don't think she realizes why he zeroed in on her. He has street skills. She's still learning.

Her background is a little jumbled, mainly because he kept interrupting, like he was trying to craft her story too. What is clear is that she was born and raised in Phoenix. When she left or was forced from there, she came to Hollywood. She met him soon after.

She started talking about how depressed she had been, and mostly still was. We were able to talk one-on-one for a few minutes as he talked to the others that had stopped by to check in. She still couldn't believe where she was. As she and I talked more, she told me they'd had a son not long before. When I asked what had happened to him, that's when he jumped back in. After listening to a long rant about how it was everyone else's fault except theirs, I found out that he had been taken away and was in foster care in Nevada.

He overrode her and started talking again. He went on a run about Big Government and the usual conspiracy crap that I associate with people who feel powerless. He then started talking about settling in Hollywood when the gangs were working together to take back the streets. I asked him if he was talking about The Guardian Angels or a group like them and he just looked confused. I interrupted to get him back on track some, too late though, as all the stories he shared then were bullshit.

***

I steered him back again and talked about day-to-day survival. They each get one hundred dollars a month in food stamps. They immediately sell those. She gets two-hundred-twenty-five dollars a month in either Welfare or Disability. That was unclear, though I lean toward Welfare. They don't use that to get off the street, but to stay on it. They know which organizations hand out food and most anything else they might need. They also know when and where. They get free medical care at the clinic. The money they've cashed in or gotten pays for his weed, cigarettes, the Pepsi he likes so much, and other daily things they want. His begging augments it. At our next meeting I was going to get to watch him in action.

***

I met him early the next day in front of a popular diner off Hollywood Boulevard. He has crafted his homeless and hungry sign onto a kid's fishing pole he found in the trash. He put a cup on the hook and he lets it out as people pass then reels it in when they put money in it. He thinks he's witty and amusing. I sat with him for about an hour during the early rush. I shook my head as he counted out twenty-seven dollars and thirty-three cents. A good morning for him. Enough for a little weed, some cigarettes, and a couple of Pepsis. That was also just the early shift, he would go back again later. Let me explain this straight. Don't give homeless people money. Whatever story they tell you isn't true. I can give you a bunch of lines and stories, from all the people I've talked to, but any money goes for what they desire, not something they need. One group thought they were smart and decided to give out gift cards instead. No. No. No. They sell those too. Anything that can be sold, is.

After his morning work, we headed to the 7-11 for his cigarettes then back to the building alcove where they had slept the night before. He handed his street wife a Pepsi and also a honeybun that he had gotten her as a treat. He gave me an ingratiating look as he told me he took such good care of her. Yeah, probably not.

He fell asleep soon after. No doubt worn out from his morning's work. The sun was up by then and it had been a chilly Hollywood night, so I asked the wife if she wanted to walk with me for a bit and get some sun. She looked back to make sure he was sleeping and then quietly nodded yes.

Even though she lived on the streets, I don't think she really even noticed a lot of the cool urban art and other neat things that were surrounding her. We walked over by Hollywood High School and talked about the mural of graduates painted on its front. I told her my favorite was Judy Garland as Dorothy. We started talking about the different people and she had this immature view that all their lives were so glamorous. I talked some about what I did know. As I spoke about Carol Burnett, I told her that she should go to the library and read her autobiography about growing up poor in Hollywood. The wife was completely dispirited. I don't think positive influence in her life had ever been in the forefront. She had graduated high school so that was a good start. She's not stupid, she just has no self-confidence. Being on the street has dropped that even lower. We sat on the low wall by the school and talked for probably an hour about different organizations that would do most any and everything they could to help her in any way she needed. I told her to quit looking at everything as a way to scam it and instead look at those organizations for the true reason they were there, to help people who need them. I added that he did his own thing and slept a lot and she could surely find time to go talk to people. Then I also added that if she was scared to go against him that she may want to wonder why. I then said that there were shelters she could go to for that very reason. We eventually got up and started heading back, with a detour to 7-11 for coffee.

When we got there, he was awake and mad. As a controller of everything, he proved my thoughts as he berated her for going off on her own. Usually a watcher, I stepped in. Since they had allowed me to hear their story, I figured I had the right. I actually told him to shut his fucking mouth. I think he was stunned more than anything. I was holding her hand as I spoke to him to pass on good energy. Her hand was shaking as I called him out on all his bullshit.

After he calmed down, I sat and listened for a while as he told more tales of his romantic life on the streets. I didn't even bother to write them down, since they weren't true either. I stayed to let her settle and to distract him for a while.

One truth that he did share was that the street is just as addictive as any drug. No responsibility, no anything. Do whatever you want, act however you please. He's right too. From the research I have done, I have found that about eighty percent of homeless are there by choice, by addiction, by mental illness, and by escape. Or a combination of those things. Of that other twenty percent, half of them want to get off the street but want you to do the work. The remaining half are working their asses off to change their life.

My Thoughts and Views

I don't like him. Not one little bit. After a few days of thought, it really is that simple. He is a predator. He is a user. He is a bum. You can see it in his eyes. You can hear it in his bullshit. His life isn't romantic or adventurous. It's just his choice.

<u>The Hillbilly</u>

SW Florida. We met as we waited at the same bus stop for the 2. We were both headed downtown. When we got off at the same place, we realized we were both also headed to the library. We continued our first conversation there.

***

She was born in the West Virginia Appalachians or as she says, the boonies outside of the sticks in the Appalachians of southern West Virginia. She smiles when she says that.

Not much outlook, not much hope. When you look at the world around you, all you see is poor, poorer, and poorest. She says it's so easy to not see how beautiful the mountains are when all you see is a trap.

Every generation of her family that she knows of, worked in coal. Somewhat offhand, she says that some died by accident, some by black lung, and some had it worse, they lived.

She can remember when she was little that her father would make it home, exhausted, and go into the outside shower they had. Black with coal, he wouldn't come in the house until it was washed away.

***

She is thirty-two now but seems older somehow. As we talked, she told me that even when she was little, she knew the world she lived in was not the one she wanted. She always daydreamed of sunlight, warm breezes and blue water. She added that by eight she knew, somehow, she would have exactly that. Even then she knew how hard that was going to be.

When she was younger, she would do whatever nickel, dime, or quarter jobs that her mother or others would find for her. She never spent any of it; she hid it from the beginning.

She says she sounds like a typical hillbilly when she talks about her family. When I asked her to list them off, she took a deep breath as I smiled. "Okay. Let's see. Daddy, Mama, three brothers, two sisters, I'm next to oldest. Um, twenty-two first cousins that I know of, eight sets of aunts and uncles, Granny and Papa, and my other grandparents passed already." I asked her if they were close by. She nodded to herself as she answered, "Too close. Most all of us lived on the same land." I love listening to her talk. I have a southern accent but hers is way past that. I mentioned my thoughts and she said, "Yep. Dead country. I need to take a class or something." We both laughed.

I asked about education. She was nodding along again. "Definitely. From day one, I was teacher's pet. I usually didn't want to go home." I asked her about the rest and she said that she was the first in her family, that she knew of, to graduate high school. "I got picked on a bunch. Teacher's pet. Snob. Stuck up. Butt kisser. Think I'm better than everybody. Too good for the jobs around there. You name it, I probably heard it." I asked if she ever responded. "Nope. Don't get me wrong. Sometimes it would hurt my feelings or make me mad, but I knew what I wanted and they didn't. I think they were scared more than anything, truthfully." I agreed as she continued, "Most everybody else was done by fourteen. Fifteen latest. I don't know the statistics, but I think our three-county area had to be one of the highest. Probably worse now."

Since she is, in fact, thirty-two now, I asked what she did after she graduated. "Felt guilty. Stupid, but I did. I stayed to try and help. That was dumb. No helping what is. I got a job in the dollar store in town and worked as many hours as they'd give me. I rented a room from a nice town lady, a widow. Same job, same place the whole time I was there. I really got called names then. People told me I needed to find a husband, all my sisters and brothers were married, have babies, make a life. Well, I didn't want a husband and surely wasn't bringing a baby into that, and I was making a life, they just didn't know it."

I asked her when she finally thought she had enough money saved to go. She answered quickly, "Never. I never did, but I left anyway." I asked why. "That's easy. One word. Meth."

She talked about just how terrible it was. She had thought coal was bad enough, but this was so much worse. That she watched people change from humans to hyped-up zombies. I asked about her family. "Oh, yeah. It got a bunch of them. I don't even know how many. I remember that my Papa used to tell me stories about the old days of moonshining and how they knew the law was coming before they got there. The same thing is happening now. They catch some but not enough. It's bad."

I asked her how she made her way here. She smiled, "Library, computer, Trailways."

I laughed too, then asked about the shelter. "I got here when the snow bird people were here and couldn't find a place in what I figured my price range was. Not one that I would stay in anyway, so I came here." She went on to say how kind everyone was and that it wasn't like many people thought it was. "It's not drunks and junkies. Those kind of people aren't allowed to come in, except to eat. The people that stay for any length of time are starting over and either working or looking for work. I do a little volunteer stuff with them a couple of days a week, the others I come here." I asked her about the time limit and she said for those few days she had to be out that she stayed in one of the trail motels.

As our first interview ended, I asked her what she liked the best about being here. Quietly, she answered, "Everything. Every single thing. But, that's not what you asked so if I had to pick one, it would be walking on the beach."

***

I met her at the library again. She looked up and smiled as I walked up. I said, "Come on. We'll miss the bus." "To where?" "Let's rock the beach, girl. Come on." She smiled and got up.

As we were riding, we were both quiet, but she had a huge grin on her face. When we got off and walked out onto the beach, she turned and said, "This is really nice. Thank you. I never would have thought to do this by myself." I winked, and we kept walking. We managed to hit as the tide was going out and I told her about some of the history I did know as we went along. She was really enjoying herself, just picking up shells and breathing it in. I took a couple of phone pictures as we went.

After we had walked for a while, we found a patch of sand and sat down. She smiled and said, "This is just nice. A perfect celebration." I asked what we were celebrating, and her entire face lit up. "I got a job. They hired me. I am so happy." A tear leaked out as I congratulated her. "That is awesome. Where?" She laughed. "Right back where I started, a dollar store." "Awesome again. I bet you make shift leader in a month." "I hope so, but that's not all." I looked at her. "The church place is helping me get into an apartment. I went and saw it yesterday. It's cute." I congratulated her again. Her eyes sprung a leak again as she quietly said, "I can't believe it's all happening. I've wanted this since I was eight years old. I can't even find the words I want." I told her I understood completely. We hung out for a while, chatting with small talk, and then off the beach to catch the bus back downtown.

She told me she would be staying at the shelter until she got her first two paychecks and that the apartment rent would be based on her income. "I told them I had been saving but they said to keep right on doing that." She said they liked to hear things like that and went on to tell her that they knew she was going to be one of their success stories. I told her she already was. She just smiled again.

I asked if she had been in contact with her family or if she would be now. She told me she was still thinking on it. "They were happy enough to see me go. They were mad. I know it's because they were hurting and because they didn't understand." When I asked her to amplify on that, she said that I had to understand how they thought. That they were brought up to only see what was right in front of them. She added, "It's kind of like they didn't know they had other choices."

I told her that she was brave and a lot stronger than I bet she knew. She laughed. "Thank you. I know I'm tough. I had to be around all those hillbillies." I laughed as she continued, "But sometimes, on my bad days you know, I wasn't sure I could do it."

I told her if she was unsure about her family that she didn't have to talk to them yet. She could just write a nice letter to her parents and let them know how she was doing. I told her to take a couple of pictures of herself, the beach, or whatever, and send those with it. She laughed again. "I don't have a phone yet, I surely don't have a camera, and they don't have a computer either. I said, "Let's go have a photo shoot then. I'll take some pictures and we can get them printed at Walgreen's. That way you can send some and keep some." She told me she didn't have any since she had gotten here. I told her she'd be styling and profiling and her family would think she was a bigtime model now. She blushed and said, "I'm surely not pretty enough for that." I told her that she was but it's what showed inside of her and her attitude that people would see. "Do you think so?" "Yep. Let's rock it, supermodel. Come on."

We took a leisure walk down to the bayfront then spent about thirty minutes taking pictures. She watched as I cleaned them up and then emailed them to the drug store. As we were parting for the day, I told her I'd bring them to our next meeting before she started her new job on Monday. She smiled and said, "Can I hug you? This has been an amazing day."

***

For our last meeting, we decided to walk down the hill to the bay and sit on one of the uncomfortable benches and watch the day come alive. After we got settled and before we really started talking, I unzipped my bag and pulled out all the pictures. I handed them to her without comment. Her smile was huge as she started flipping through them. She looked up at me and said, "These came out so good. You made me look really nice." I laughed and told her she did look nice and that if she thought my (lack of) camera skills had anything to do with it, she was wrong. She smiled and said, "I agreed with you about something." I joked that was probably dangerous. She shook her head and said, "Stop. I'm serious. I've been working on a letter to my parents. These will be great to put in. Do you want to see it?" I told her I would if she wanted me to, but I didn't want to get all in her personal business. Without a word, she handed me the letter then continued looking at the pictures. I read quietly. She had done a great job. As I handed it back to her, I told her so. "Thank you. I was nervous. I think I still want them to think good of me." I told her that I was sure, no matter what occurred, that in reality, they were very proud of her. She smiled again and said, "Do you really think so?" I told her I most definitely did.

We talked for a little while about what or what might not be going on in West Virginia and then I asked her if she was excited to start her new job in the morning. She nodded. "I really am. Very much so. Like I told you the other day, sometimes on my bad days I think I felt a little depressed or worried." I told her she was going to do great and that after a week, they'd wish she would have come sooner. I joked that I lived not too far from where she'd be, so I'd have to come in and harass her. She laughed. "You'd better. I mean it." She told me about the new things the shelter had provided so she'd have good work clothes and shoes, the bus pass she had been given, and all the other things they'd helped her with. She then said, "I made up my mind too." When I asked about what, she answered, "Once I get going good and get settled in my new apartment, I'm going to volunteer there. I'm going to start out at one day a week." I told her that was really cool, and she added, "It's the least I can do. I couldn't have done all this without them."

We talked more about her time at the shelter then I asked her about her apartment and she went on to tell me that it wasn't just the place, but they were helping her with everything she needed to go in it as well. She seemed surprised. I said, "When you get settled, get in touch with me. I'll come take pictures of that for you too." She looked at me then and said, "I had already decided that you're going to be my first guest. You'll come for dinner, won't you?" I told her I wouldn't miss it for the world. And that I was probably as happy for her as she was.

We talked for a while about her family, her new life, and her excitement about everything happening now. I knew our interviews were done. I did something I don't often do. I looked over at her and said, "Well, you're stuck with me now. You are one of mine and I really do care about how you're doing. If you need anything or you just want to talk, get in touch and I'll be there." Her eyes teared as she said, "Really? You mean it?" She hugged me tight as I said, "I do. I wouldn't be anywhere else." I reminded her of our promised dinner date, hugged her back, and then we got up to head back up the hill.

My Thoughts and Views

She is a really neat person and stronger than I think even she understands. Raised in a world to only see limited options, she saw more.

Her work ethic in obtaining her goals shows a lot about the kind of person she is. But, within that, she never lost her kindness or joy, nor her care for others.

Her goals may seem small to many, but they're not. Some people search their entire life to find satisfaction and happiness, she envisioned from early on what that would be and worked to find it. She's pretty terrific. And she's almost there.

<u>The White Russian</u>

SE Florida. We met because I was laughing to myself. If anyone ever looked out of place at a bus station, it was her. I was standing out on the sidewalk while deciding which bus I was going to hop on when she pulled up and parked her Mercedes Maybach across the street. She got out looking irritated and a little confused. I asked if she needed help and she told me that she was picking up a guy doing some painting at one of her properties. She sensed I wasn't one of 'those people' so she sat down with me to wait for him. We chatted about this and that for a while.

***

She is a White Russian. Not really. But her parents were. She was actually born after they immigrated here during the Purge. That era of Russian history is fascinating. Her grandparents were members of the Whites. Those were the people loyal to the Tsar. When the revolution came, that went out of favor, then during the Civil War that began that same year, the, by then, Reds went after the Whites (and the Greens). Over three million died and she has family members that did. Her parents were small children during this time. When Lenin died, and Stalin eventually came to power, after a time, the Purges begin. That would be anyone that was an "enemy" or had been a member of an opposition party. More of her family disappeared then too. By the end of that period, her parents were married, and they made plans to flee. They made it out in the thirties, just as the world was heading toward war again. It was time for the guy's bus to get there and I told her that I had really enjoyed talking, explained what I was doing, and asked her if she wanted to talk more. She said yes but it would have to be the next weekend. She gave me time and place as I thanked her and got up to catch the bus I decided on.

We met at a waterfront park and found a spot at a table under a gazebo. Not much of a social conversationalist, she is very serious. That is true. She was born when her parents were in their forties and she is an only child. Although she has a quiet sense of humor and is actually rather funny, not many people see that side. It wasn't really encouraged when she was young. Her parents equated success with Capitalism. They embraced it and taught her that professional success and accumulation of wealth defined their class. She said that they had brought that White Russian elitism with them to this country and were still very rigid in their belief of social class. They were snobs. Poor when they arrived, it didn't matter because they were people of society and carried themselves that way.

She speaks with a bit of an accent, but it's from being around them. It's very faint but leads most to believe she is a foreigner though she grew up in Miami, the original southern melting pot of peoples and cultures.

She was always successful in school. She didn't dare not be. She said that she often felt forty when around the other kids. They were full of fun and frivolity and she had her nose in a book. A lot of them. Her parents had decided that she should be a doctor and from an early age, that's the path she followed. She can remember other little girls telling her she had to be a nurse when asked what she wanted to be when she grew up.

I asked if she had childhood friends and she did. But she said other than one, they were all a lot like her. Very studious and serious. I told her they were nerds. She laughed quietly and said yes, but they didn't have that word then. She also added that for a girl in the US in the late fifties and early sixties that had higher professional aspirations, a serious temperament had to be worn, much like a mask, to dissuade anyone, particularly men, from wanting to pat her on the head and tell her to be a good girl. By the look on her face, I'm sure that happened a lot. When I asked, she said it did, but usually only once. She smiled then. She has a great one but doesn't use it often enough. I went back to the friend that was different and she smiled again. She told me that she was everything she wasn't. She was so American. She was silly, she was pretty, she was fun, she was nice, and she was popular. She has no idea why they were friends but said she dragged her right into the mix with her and was the only one that could ever get her to act that way too.

We went back to her schooling. She was very proud of herself. By then, her parents were in their sixties. She graduated as valedictorian, the first girl in her school's history. She said her parents sat on the front row at graduation with very serious faces and their noses in the air. She had already been accepted to Miami, with a partial scholarship for academics.

I asked about college then medical school and if she ever had college fun. Once again, she said she didn't have time for that, she had a lot to get done and achieve. However, her same friend would come and visit, then drag her off for some silliness somewhere. I said that she was lucky that she had someone like that in her life and then asked if they were still in contact. She told me that she had gone into real estate, which was perfect for her and her personality. She was very successful and even now, still carried that girlish glee. She said that she had no choice to be friends still She said her friend wouldn't have allowed her not to be. She smiled again, and I told her she liked it. She said she did.

We headed to relationships then. She admitted that was the one area of her life where she was not a success. She told me that she didn't have her first date until medical school. She was twenty-four. Even then, it was more of a group thing. She went out with him again alone and dated him for a while, but she didn't want any distraction to break her focus or distract her from her goals.

I asked how that translated after school was done and she said she just wasn't very good at it. She wasn't good at small talk and didn't pretend to be. As I watch her, she has that same inbred snobbery that her parents had. I told her that probably made many keep their distance. She agreed and said often she did it on purpose to make them do that. I told her besides doctor and daughter, she was a woman and at some point, she had to have said, "Hmmm, let's give that a try." She laughed out loud and I smiled. I had snuck that one in on her. She really does have a great smile and laugh.

She said that she had been married four times. I told her she was competing with the Gabor sisters. She said in each instance, the man was handsome and intelligent, but in the end, they were men. She made a face of her thoughts on that. She said that each seemed attracted to her because she was intelligent and successful, but as soon as she got in a real relationship with them, they did nothing but try to change her so they could be "the man." Eventually she divorced each of them. And quit trying. She says that she still dates, even now, but leaves it at a very surface level.

I can see men wanting to crack the ice and thinking it might be worth it. She is actually very attractive and keeps herself incredibly fit. Even though she wouldn't admit it, she knows it too. She did say that marriage number two was worth it though, because it gave her a daughter. When I asked about her, she told me that she is a doctor too.

I asked her about her medical school experiences. She said that educationally, she was motivated and excited by what she was learning. She went on to add that the rest wasn't so great. She started medical school in 1972 and was one of only three women in her class. She tells me that it was a boys' club all the way and that sexual harassment and other forms of intimidation were not only okay, they were expected. She felt like it was often the goal of those with frat boy mentalities to make them quit. I asked how she handled that, and she said that the three of them, though dissimilar, made a pledge to always display a united front. She said that it doesn't sound like much, but whenever there was one, there was three. She said that cowards will pick on one but will not usually take on three, so they stuck together like glue through their time together. She said the pressure was still there, the intimidation was too, but they had each other and that helped a lot. I told her that sisterhood was powerful, and she answered that she may not have made it through without it. She finished in the top ten of her class and once again, her parents were there in the front row with their noses in the air. I asked about her classmates and she said that both had graduated and were still successful physicians as well.

We moved to her internship. She said although this sounds somewhat like a stereotype that she chose to go north for that as she thought she would be treated more equally and have the space to truly hone her craft. When I asked if it was true, she said yes and no. She went on to explain that interns were worked so hard and usually completely exhausted, so they really didn't have the energy for immature medical school shenanigans, but every once in a while, something ignorant would occur, though it was isolated and not the norm. When she was done, she was offered a residency back in Florida, so she came home.

She also adds that by that time some views were starting to change. It was the time of feminists and the women's movement and her time in her residency was much more relaxed than either medical school or her internship had been. When she finished that final hurdle, she stayed and went on staff at the same hospital.

Because she is so reserved, it is hard to get her to talk about herself as a person. I went back to her parents. I said that we had only talked about them briefly and then mostly with humor, but I would like to know a little more about them as people.

She said that her father had been a jeweler in Russia. When they fled, he managed to sneak out a few of his better stones. They had hidden some and sewn others into clothes. When they first arrived in Miami, there was only a smaller Russian community and it was made by people much like her parents. She added that other Russian minorities congregated in New York and other areas. Back to her story, she said that they took about a year to meet people and get assimilated to the American way of life and then he found a little shop that was available and opened a small storefront here. I told her that she had great taste in jewelry and she said she had learned all of it from her father. She went on to say that by the time he stopped working, he had three successful shops. I asked what he was like as a person and she said that he was quiet and studious but friendly. I told her she had just described herself. She agreed and said in temperament, she was much like him. She told me that he died just near the end of the last century and that seemed right, since he had been born near the beginning of it. Quietly, she added that she missed him still.

When I moved to her mother. She smiled. "Dragon lady." When I asked her why, she said everyone was scared of her and called her that behind her back. She also added that she knew and liked the title. I asked what she had done. She said that she held court. Salons, readings, art, music, whatever caught her fancy at the time. She said as a child she watched quietly as all kinds of people sat at her mother's feet in their living room and listened with rapt attention as she expounded on any number of subjects. She said she acted like she was Catherine the Great, and I laughed. I asked after her and she said that she had died only a couple of years before, well into her nineties. And that she had still held court until she couldn't anymore.

We talked more about her daughter next. Of her, she is very proud. Much like her parents, she was born later. She was in her mid-thirties when she had her. They became the two musketeers and were as much friends as mother and daughter and that was often still true. She added that she has a very good balance of American and Russian personality and outlook and that her patients loved her. She is a pediatrician. I asked if she was ready to be a grandma and she said that her daughter was following family tradition with that and wasn't ready for that part of her life yet.

I asked when she had decided to go into private practice. She tells me that she stayed at the hospital until she felt she had enough experience and had learned enough then she sought out her place in the medical field. Where her practice is now, is where it started. She has patients that were children of her original patients now too. She is quietly traditional as well. And likes it.

I asked her about her personal likes and we talked for quite a while about those. I think she probably doesn't get to share much of this very often.

She loves flowers and with the great weather here, grows orchids. She took out her phone and showed me pictures of some of her favorites. Obviously, those are another talent of hers. The ones she shared are healthy and beautiful.

She also enjoys decorating as her form of art expression and meticulously plans out her themes and styles for her homes, of which she has three.

She likes fast cars and says she drives like a Russian. That made her smile and laugh. I had seen her car and could see where she could get in trouble. She adds that she's never gotten a ticket. She pulls out her credentials and says she is on her way to an emergency. They always let her go. I told her that was cheating, and she laughed.

Her music tastes are mixed, and she has a good understanding of the complexities of classical works. She says that to her, that genre is relaxing.

I asked her what she did to let off steam and she says that she very much enjoys yardwork and as far as exercise, she does kick boxing. I told her I could envision her beating both her yard and opponents into submission. That one, she liked. She laughed and laughed as we ended our time together.

My Thoughts and Views

Although she shows mostly ice, she is a woman of many passions. In her work, she cares deeply about her patients. Obviously, many agree since she has had a thriving practice for about thirty years now. To those she has allowed into her world, whether they be close friends or family, that care is the same.

Also, not admitted but true, she is a feminist. She has spent her life making her place in a, at first, male-dominated profession. By keeping her focus on her final goal, she did not allow the mundanities of the day-to-day experiences to win.

As for her personal life and its lack of success, she says that is more her than them at this point. She has her ways and routine and likes her solitary life just fine. At the times she wants to be social, she is comfortable and enjoys herself.

She is also a success in the world as envisioned by her parents. She is a very good physician and she is also very wealthy now. Again, she is comfortable with both.

In the end, she is completely comfortable with who she is. Her reserve is part of her while also sometimes being the mask she mentioned. When she takes it off, she is personable, intelligent, and funny. I enjoyed meeting her.

<u>The Pretty Little Liar</u>

Coastal South Carolina. We met at the downtown bus station. As I basically watched her pitch a fit on the phone and then work into a full-fledged snit when the call ended, I laughed to myself but was in the mood to play so I walked up and introduced myself.

She is definitely one of those people who pretends to be way too good to ride public transportation. She was mad because no one else she tried to call realized her life was much more important than theirs. I made it easy for her. I told her that she had to ride two buses to get where she was going and that she'd have to wait about thirty minutes until the first was back and then ready to go again. I told her if she wanted, I'd sit with her. She liked me because I gave her the attention she knew she deserved and confided that she was going to have an anxiety attack riding a bus with those kind of people. I thought to myself that this was going to be really interesting so I offered to ride with her as she headed for the dealership to pick up her imported sports car.

By the time the first bus was ready to go, we were fast, fake friends. She actually agreed to be interviewed because everyone would really see how beautiful, professional, talented, intelligent, amazing and fabulous she was. She was excited to share stories of her perfect life, perfect career, and perfect family. That's paraphrasing some but not much.

***

She's is a textbook narcissist and completely self-involved. No matter the situation, she makes it about her. She backstabs and worse. She practices alternative history. If she walks in on a conversation, she jumps right in and makes up her part in it, or similar things that she's done or had done. She has to be the center of attention. She's beautiful. Nobody likes her. Not really. She doesn't like herself. At all.

***

She works in the public eye. There, she loves everybody. They are all her best friends. She's so interested in what you have to say or what you're doing. Every bit of her attention is on you. Of course, off camera, she is texting her friends and trashing you. Her voice sounds a little fake, but maybe that's just the way she talks? Her eyes look a little crazy. Hmmm....

***

She is completely capable of seeing and knowing only what she chooses. If something is happening right in front of her, or someone says something, if it's not something she wants to know or admit then she simply pretends she didn't hear or see. I've wondered if she realizes that others see that? Probably. But she pretends she doesn't. Because it's easier.

***

Fake. Shallow. Mean. She doesn't even admit those parts of her to herself. She can't accept that she does those things because then she'd have to admit why. She's not ready to do that yet. Maybe, she never will be. In the meantime, she works to make most as miserable as she is. She seeks attention and definition from others. When they can't give her what she needs, or they reveal their humanity, or they disappoint or hurt her, well, bad things will happen to good people. It's too close to the pain. She fights against feeling it.

Self-protection. Self-preservation. Self-esteem. Sense of self. What are those? And who is she? Really?

***

She interested me quite a bit. She craved the attention. And I spent a week really getting to know her and about two months after I'd come home, talking to her on the phone or emailing with her. I became somewhat immersed in her world during that week as she introduced me to her friends and family. I also got many of their numbers so they could tell me how great she was too. Of course, they didn't. They eventually shared their true thoughts and memories. They go from her early years to the present. Most portrayed her as a master manipulator. And I'm sure she is. But they have to allow it since it always takes two. It doesn't make her happy, nothing does. But she thinks it gives her control. It doesn't.

***

She is in her late thirties and from a smaller town about half way between where she lives now and the state capital. A town where everyone knows everyone. She told me that she has been abandoned by everyone she's ever loved. Others told me that in many or most cases, she, or her actions, gave that a push, even when she was young.

Her birth father left when she was young; somewhere around the fifth grade. To this day, he pretends that he never had a first family. He finds that simpler than dealing with the person she is. She is invisible to him. He still lives in that small town and if she's in town and at an event where he is, he doesn't even know her. She'll walk up to his group and introduce herself, wanting that acknowledgement, and the people she speaks to will say things like, "I didn't realize he had another daughter." He stays silent. Her heart is broken again. But that's mainly because she fakes those emotions for others so she can get attention. She doesn't really feel bad, only tries to work the situation for how it makes her look.

Her mother, she describes as a dramatic hypochondriac. She jokes, though it's not funny. She also adds that she may be those things, but she's the only one that's never left her. That's all she knows. Of course, that story changes too, depending on what she's trying to get out of it at the time. She and her mother are very much alike.

***

As a young adult, all she wanted was to feel safe and loved. She wanted to be in control. She made a box for herself (in her head) of what the perfect life would be. Then she worked hard to fill it. It didn't matter that people are human. It really didn't matter who it was. They were going to fit in her box. Of course, you can't put people in a box.

She met who would become the husband not long after high school. She had been dumped by her high school boyfriend at that point though I won't share what she did to him to get even. But, back to the husband-to-be. He was a little older than her, had already been married, had a son already, and he was a dick. Didn't matter. She was putting him in the box. She was already behind though. She was number three in his world.

For years, she formed her box. The part that gets left out of that story is that not long after they married, he joined the Army and was sent to basic training not too far from their hometown. From the day he got there, she was on it. Whenever she could, she would drive up there, she also got anyone and everyone's phone numbers and would call them obsessively when she was working and couldn't get there. Long story short, he was given a medical discharge at the end of basic training. I'm sure the military was relieved to be rid of that, but she had what she wanted. He was now home where he could give her the attention she had to have. Although murky, next he was in law enforcement although I have no details. Do I need to tell you how that ended? But that gets left out too.

Needless to say, he cheated on her from the beginning. In the box, you don't see things like that because they don't fit. He is also an alcoholic. Who wouldn't be? But I digress because the big deal came next. The child. This was her true chance for salvation. She was going to be the Perfect Mother and have the Perfect Child. She was going to make her daughter just like her. Perfect.

Sidetrack a little. In case you can't tell, she was already a little nuts. Still mostly hiding it unless you dealt with her daily or you had hurt her or her family. Small animals, job losses, random things. But those didn't fit in the box either. She is also overly dramatic and a hypochondriac like her mother, though not to that extreme. She'd never admit it though. It's that see and hear what you want to thing again.

No matter what, through the years, that box was going to stay intact. Duct tape, super glue, whatever it took. Still didn't really matter that the real world didn't fit. Of course, everything takes two. Yes, her husband was a dick, but really, so was she. Both of them did everything and anyone they chose, drank, whatever. Didn't matter. Box was still holding. This is also when the revisionist history really started. She could look someone in the face and completely rewrite anything. Didn't matter that they had been right there with her and knew the truth. If she repeated it the way she wanted it to be enough times, it would become the real truth. That box thing again.

Anyway, her daughter became the second coming. She had someone to mold to be just like her. But that was then; now her daughter is a young lady. At this point, she doesn't even talk to her. She has always had to be in control of everything. Otherwise, how can she craft a situation so it's about her? Micro-managing, molding what people see, revising everything. Funny though, she says she loves her like nothing else. But even that usually only shows in who she is as a reflection of her. Still, the daughter hates her a lot right now. She's in her early twenties, lives as far away as she could get, and has a husband. However, she knows best. She used to call and tell them exactly what to do. They finally realized they didn't have to answer and now just don't. Her daughter has left her for another. Of course, what that means is that she's starting a teaching career and is working to start to build a family of her own. That's not what she sees since she has to control that too. She sees that her husband is a controlling jerk and has turned her against her.

***

I have to sidetrack a little again. After her daughter graduated high school, her husband left her. That's what she'll tell you. It's somewhat convoluted but there was drama and bad acts on both sides so it was actually kind of mutual. He was exhausted by her, because, well, who wouldn't be? It ended up that she called his bluff during a blowout argument. Her rages are something to see. Anyway, during one of them, she actually left him. Oops. She had been having a long-term affair of her own. That rewriting history thing again. Always the victim.

He also has a new girlfriend and has for a while. I've heard from others that she's nice. I'm actually surprised she hasn't killed her somehow, either metaphorically or for real. The funny thing is, she doesn't actually care. She really doesn't. She just doesn't like that someone else was picked over her. That's something she'll never stand for.

And, she won't divorce him. She really doesn't like him, or herself, they had a terrible marriage, he's an alcoholic, he thinks she's crazy. On and on. But, in her dramatic moments, and with a straight face, she tells you that they will always be together. He will barely talk to her, only if he absolutely has too, and won't answer phone calls or texts unless it gets to be a crazier crazy than her usual crazy. She rants, raves, screams, and kicks. If I was him, I'd move and change my number. I'm not defending him. Just from talking to him, I think he's an asshole. But, again, so is she. Plus, the rest. But back to what I was saying, they've been separated for about four years. That box is raggedy as hell, but it's still that box. If she throws it away, or lets it completely fall apart, then what? Only problem is that it never was intact and is gone now. She just can't let it go. She'll do whatever needed to keep the facade.

***

Every single person I spoke with mentioned this. She invents close ties. She likes drama and tragedy. If someone dies, they were her closest friend in the world. As she goes on, you realize that you've never heard their name mentioned. Not once. She also hops on social media then and eulogizes them while building up her own important role in their life and how close they were.

She does that same thing with other family and friends. It's situational. If there is a drama, she is on it. These people mean the world to her, whoever they are. You surely haven't heard of them. She all of a sudden will gain a god-brother, god-sister, second cousin, best friend from school, home, or wherever. You're still just shaking your head as you're thinking to yourself, who? As soon as the crisis or greatness passes, you will never hear about them again. But in the moment that person is her only focus as she amplifies her role in their life. Her writings go on for a page sometimes. There's almost as many of those as there are pictures of herself.

***

Because I spent so much time with her during that week and then on the phone and I am not connected to her historically or emotionally, I can see all the different sides of who she is. It's funny, not particularly ha-ha, but at her best she is beautiful, she is self-depreciating, she is funny. Right now, it doesn't come out often. Mostly not at all. The rest of her time is spent in this terrible swirl of pettiness, drama, anger, meanness and obnoxious 'I know best' mode. It's exhausting. Unless it's for an event with others or for her work, she doesn't leave the house. She hangs out on her bed all day. That's not an exaggeration. That phone is in her hand as she calls people, texts them, and posts stuff. She hides from the real world but is lost if she can't do the other three. It's tiring but she always seems pleased as she sits and tells everyone else what to do and how great she is from her throne.

***

She has no clue who she really is. She's never had to be just her. Her definition has always been by how others perceive her. She is terrified, afraid, and alone with her thoughts. When the crazy gets her, when she's really afraid, that's when you see the actions we've talked about. Her emotions are also very immature. No example of how to deal with stuff. Everything is a drama. Reactions are to the extreme, one way or the other. She has no gray area in her life. It is either black or white.

She goes back to her hometown often and tortures everyone in it. Because it's small, she practiced on them from an early age and the easy ones fall right in line. She says she hates it there, but it's the only place she can control to some extent.

Since she lives in a much bigger city now, she can only manipulate an individual or situation in spurts there. They might play for a bit and that's it. She has to go to her hometown to feel powerful. At the same time, she needs the bigger city so she can lie about how loved she is there to all the people back home. Added to that, if she can't get home and starts getting crazy, she calls everyone and tortures them that way. Simple advice. Don't answer. If you do, you're as culpable as she is.

My Thoughts and Views

She intrigued me in a lot of different ways. I don't like her, not really. She is incredibly unlikeable. I've watched as she's done or said cruel and mean things to or about so many. She always seems pleased when she's stirred something up. I would see a brief glimmer of who she can be now and then but those instances were few and far between.

The person she is now really isn't very likeable to anyone else either. I have talked to so many people from her life.

The story they've painted has helped to see her more in-depth as they've amplified events and actions that have occurred throughout.

I thought about the nature versus nurture with her too. I also did research into narcissistic and histrionic personalities. She'd be pleased that she aced the test on both. I believe that most of her narcissism comes from nature and was amplified by nurture. The histrionics are definitely from nurture.

The Free Bird

Alabama. We met at the downtown depot while she was waiting for the 12. She was going to visit a client in the hospital and said it was easier to ride there than try to park.

***

She is a black woman adopted and raised by white, Jewish parents. She is also a convicted felon and an ex-con who understood her choices and mistakes and vowed when she landed in prison to change her life and then do the same for others.

***

She was born to a young woman with drug issues. The parental rights were rescinded at her birth and she was moved to foster care and put up for adoption. She was adopted when she was three months old by the couple that had fostered her since birth. They are her parents.

She says that when she was little, she didn't realize that her family was different. It was when school started that the names and questions started. She adds that her parents were awesome and spoke to her easily about any and everything. She always felt safe, secure, and loved.

She didn't really start acting out until near the end of junior high. Martin Luther King was killed and she was trying to understand her heritage and black identity. She adds still that her parents were amazing and helped however she needed.

By high school, many of her black friends were angry, disenfranchised, and looking for an outlet to express it. She says that's when she began feeling like she was straddling two very different worlds.

Her parents' experience was the same but different. Both had lost immediate family in the Holocaust and they understood, in many ways, what she was going through.

***

In eleventh grade, she smoked her first joint. She said that moment was the beginning of her trip down the rabbit hole. Although she told her parents that she had tried it, she didn't tell them she liked it.

It didn't take long until she was hanging around with "that" crowd. And then, as she says, she got stupid. She started skipping school and lying to her parents, which was something she had never done.

By the middle of twelfth grade, she could tell they were worried. She said her attitude was terrible and she was angry but couldn't pinpoint why.

She met a guy on one of her skip days. They used to hook and hang out at various places, get high, and play spades. He was a drug dealer, but she justified it by saying it was just pot. No big deal.

All of a sudden, they were dating. Which means she was sneaking around and seeing him. She lied to her parents more.

She says, looking back, it's obvious she was having issues, but she saw it and didn't when it was happening.

The next thing she knew, she was talking to her parents and telling them she wanted to take a year off before starting college to experience life. She knew they were worried, but she said in her life, they never didn't support and love her.

Her eyes teared as she added, "Good thing too."

***

After graduation, she went off her deep end. She said she was an upper middle-class girl, not black or white, nor Christian or Jew, trying to be a bad ass.

Soon, she was mostly living with the boyfriend and she then understood he dealt a lot more than pot. He wasn't particularly nice to her either. She knew he slept around too. At that point, she didn't like herself much and just told herself she didn't care.

When she would see her parents, she couldn't even look them in the eye.

Not far into her year, she began helping him with his business. Rather, she ran drugs for him along with helping with other parts of it. She says that she was so dispirited, angry, high, and stupid. Add immature, as she had no idea they were being watched. She just thought she was being cool, having no idea what that really meant.

She was barely nineteen when she was arrested on a felony drug charge. Her entire world came crashing down in one moment.

After the initial humiliation of being arrested, booked, searched, fingerprinted, photographed, and being put in a jail jumpsuit, she was allowed her phone call. She never even hesitated. She called her parents, crying the entire time.

***

She said she still remembers that day vividly, though it's been forty-five years. She said they got there so fast. No recriminations, no anger, they were just worried about their baby.

Because she had those great parents, she made the bail set and went home. She never saw that guy again. As an aside, he did not get busted, he was away when it happened. He disappeared as quickly as he had appeared and somehow, she wasn't surprised. She was back in the arms of her family.

She says now that it took that day to realize just how lucky she was. Too late. But she says that day led her down the path she has been on ever since.

She had a great lawyer and that helped some, but it was a large amount of drugs. She couldn't even testify against the ex for any kind of consideration. Not only had he disappeared but she didn't know much about what went on anyway. She said even though the prosecutor's office knew she wasn't any kind of bigwig, she was the only one they caught, and she took the fall for them all. Even with that very good lawyer, even with all the considerations she did get, she was still sentenced to five years. She was headed to prison.

***

She said from the minute she became incarcerated, she grew up. She was completely disgusted and couldn't believe what she had allowed herself to become. She accepted every bit of help offered and her parents came every single visiting day. She vowed not to let what happened to her, happen to anyone else.

Within months, she had trustee status and was allowed to work outside the prison. She worked at McDonalds, about a mile away, five days a week. She said that helped so much. Still being a part of society instead of locked away and brooding. When I asked her about responsibility and anger, she said she never blamed anyone but herself. She'd had choices, she just made the wrong ones.

***

About a year in, she had completed another prison program and was allowed to enroll in college. She already knew that she wanted to get her degree in Social Work, and if she could swing it, a minor in Education. Her goal was to work as a social worker with a focus on educating women to not make the choices she had.

I asked about her experiences in prison and she said that although there was some of most everything you hear about, that she wasn't affected much since after her first year she was gone as much as she was there. She spent most days from one third to one half of the day outside the fence. She knows how lucky she was. I told her that she made her own luck and just as she took responsibility for her mistakes, she should take it for the good too. She smiled and told me she did in a way but without the support of so many different people, she never would have been able to accomplish what she had.

And accomplish she did. By her last year inside, she had about a semester left, she was tutoring other inmates, and she was teaching literacy.

When it came time for her to graduate from college, it was a truly big deal. She was a success story. The prison system was proud, her co-workers were proud, her parents were the proudest of them all, and the university was ecstatic. They invited her to speak at the graduation. She said she was floored but knew it was right to do it. She thought long and hard about what she wanted to say and spoke from the heart. She showed me a copy of it. She still keeps it framed and hanging in her living room to remind her what can be accomplished when you set your mind to it. Inspiring is too small of a word to describe it. He eyes teared as she told me that when she finished speaking that day, she was given a standing ovation. Led by her parents.

She still had work to get done though. She had about a month left in and she was preparing to re-enter the real world fully. She would be living with her parents. She had already been offered a job by Social Services and was excited about the future. She also had to complete all her release requirements.

She said when the day came, she felt a lot of different things. It was important to her that she thanked everyone that supported her. She spent the morning doing just that. In the early afternoon, she walked out the front door, crying and smiling. She was now a free woman. She was twenty-five.

***

For our last meeting, she invited me into her home and a little more into her life. I am sitting in an armchair and smiling as I look over at the couch where she is sitting beside her daughter. They are quite the pair. They talk together and sound as much like girlfriends as mother and daughter.

I had asked her before about adult relationships and she'd said that over the years she had dated and enjoyed the company of others at times, but her mission was too important to get distracted that way.

I pointed at her daughter now and they both laughed as I mentioned that I think that was more of a lifetime commitment than the other would have been. She nodded and smiled. Then the story began.

About ten years after she had been out and working hard, something happened that she had never considered. One of the women that she was working with was doing great and then found out she was pregnant. They started working to incorporate that in with the rest and not long after that, she also found out she was very ill. Having no close family ties nor anyone else she trusted more, she asked her if she would take care of her child when the time came. Trying to calm her and work on a more positive outlook for the future, she said that of course she would.

It turned out that her client was right. She had refused any kind of treatment so her baby could be born healthy. She gave birth to a beautiful baby girl and died three days later. She became an instant mom. And it made her happier than she ever knew she could be. I smile again as her daughter squeezes her hand and smiles.

She'd had such good examples that she knew she would also always be open and honest with her little girl. It has to be true. They are extremely close. They both say they always have been too. It was them against the world. Her daughter is twenty-nine now and a cool person in her own right. She says she had a good example. When she got up to get us beverages, I talked quietly with her and she told me how blessed they both were that they had found each other. I agreed and got up to move around a little.

When she came back in, I was standing and looking at her framed speech. I turned back and sat down then asked about her parents. She said her father had passed away about five years ago, but her mother showed no sign of slowing down at the age of ninety-one and was just as amazing now as she had always been. I told her that she must take after her then. They both smiled and laughed.

***

To meet her now and talk with her, few would ever guess her history though she doesn't hide it. It has been forty years since that day and her path continued just as she vowed. She never left Social Services, instead she chose to work in the system to affect change. She augmented that by volunteering with many, many organizations designed to help women achieve success. We talked for a long while about them all. She is quietly heroic but doesn't think so, though her daughter agrees with me too. She says she learned the hard way that the world wasn't just about her and that it takes individual commitment to make it a success.

She is retiring next month, and I mentioned that she surely wasn't going to be sitting still. As her daughter laughed out loud, she said maybe for a bit, but she still has so much to do.

We all talked for a while about all kinds of different things. They are both so intelligent that the conversation was easy and interesting. Eventually she quieted as her daughter and I continued. She's a cool person too and I enjoyed talking to her as well. They are most definitely a unit. The love is obvious, and their personalities are similar. As we continued to talk and laugh, I watched her. She was smiling to herself and it seemed like she was looking off into nothing as she remembered it all.

My Thoughts and Views

When I think of a strong woman, I see her. In every part of her world, she shows dignity, humor and commitment in each step.

She took what could have been the beginning of the end and made it a new beginning instead.

Her choice to focus on others for her entire adult life says more about the person she is than anything else.

She leads with compassion. She leads by example. And I think that says it all.

<u>The Chameleon</u>

SW Florida. We met at the downtown bus depot. She was arrogant and aloof, standing a bit away from everyone else like she was too good to be there. She had a helmet in her hand. I definitely had to find out more. She was riding the 17 to go pick up her motorcycle. She had about thirty minutes and I hadn't decided where I was going yet, so we started a conversation.

***

Truth. Lies. Truth. Lies. Our first meeting seemed at first to be a wash. She spent our entire time boasting, and after a while I just let her go. However, that night when I typed out my notes, I realized much of her truth was inside those. I delayed our second meeting a few days so I could study them more. Out of that first meeting came all the information I got later. What follows are parts of a few different meetings and conversations that we had.

***

I started meeting two by talking about her family. She told me that she didn't like any of them, even when she was very young. She thought they were all sheep and then explained what she meant. Those that just follow blindly. Of course, she thinks most people are.

She learned very early exactly how to play them like puppets. She said that it was easier than you'd think to do that. Well-mannered, she didn't act like a child. She would argue or discuss something clearly and she always won because usually they'd just give up. She didn't care either way really. If she won, she got what she wanted. If she lost, it was good practice for the next time. And she still did what she wanted anyway.

She said both parents, though her mother more so, would often just stare at her, wondering where she had come from and why she was like that. When she'd catch her doing it, she would just smile. She added that was a lot of fun.

She also points out that her mother, above the others, knew that she held her in contempt. She was also scared of who and what she was. Even when she was little. She said she could see it in her eyes.

But she went on to say that her sister was the easiest and she toyed with her their entire childhood. She added that it had been great practice and she had honed her skills by using her family. As a snarky add-on, she said she'd probably been in therapy ever since.

When I asked if she had cared about or loved any of them, she laughed at me.

***

As a brief side comment, at each of our meetings, she showed up dressed differently. Once she dressed like me which, I guess, is kind of hippie, once in a blazer and slacks, once preppy, once more like a jock, and once kind of every day or beach casual. When she dressed those certain ways, she also took on that personality. She was showing me how she could be so many different people to so many. It was eerie too. She pegged it every time.

***

Anyway, back to where I was. At our next meeting, she showed me some pictures of when she was young. Three caught my eye in particular. She didn't know why I'd asked, but she said in the first one, she was about a year; in the second, around five; and in the third, eleven. In all three, her eyes were dead. If I could see it so clearly, I wondered to myself how many others had seen it in her lifetime.

She said she could always read people. She has that gift. Adults, kids, whoever. She learned how to act with each to get exactly what she needed or wanted out of a person or situation. Just as she showed me with her fashion show, as a young person she could be the good kid, bad kid, sweet, cute, innocent, best friend, protector. Anything really.

I asked if she ever showed emotion. She said that although she is much better at those that she has taught herself to project, that she isn't a complete robot and had shared that side of herself with maybe a handful of people. But she was honest and said when she was younger and she had read someone wrong and the play didn't work, she would get upset and have a moment of acting like a child. But, in the end, that worked in her favor too because those that had seen a glimpse of the real her then questioned themselves, wondering if they'd been wrong.

Through school she went. Teacher's pet, class clown, no show, team player, whoever she chose. She said that's when she really embraced what she calls her dark side. When I asked what that meant, she said he used her magic wand, she laughed, to cull the herd. If an adult tried to control any aspect of who she was or what she wanted, she would ruin them. And that was also easier than you'd think. Her eyes at that point had not an ounce of humanity.

She gave me specific accounts of what she had done to two teachers and one assistant principal. One lost her job, one was transferred, and the other was demoted and moved. I asked how old she was, and she told me all that happened in junior high school. But she did add that the one teacher who she went after felt the remnants for years. I asked why, and she said that through her early twenties, whenever she needed a service or wanted something she couldn't get because of her age, she just gave her name, address and phone number and became ghost her on paper. At my look, she said to think about when we were kids. She's four years younger than me. No internet, no quick way to check anything, plus she usually did it on the phone and could sound however she wanted to. She laughed as she said that woman probably received bills she knew nothing about for ten years. She was smiling and shaking her head as she finished the story by saying, "I guess they learned their lesson."

I asked if she ever got in trouble for anything growing up. She said once in a while, for regular kid stuff. She had to throw in times of normal behavior to keep them on their toes. She added that for any big stuff, she always got out of it by playing the part needed or just ignoring it. She said the second worked great because it made people nervous since she had zero respect for their authority. She used a serious voice when she said that and then laughed out loud.

When she stopped, she said that her favorite thing then was to shoplift. No one ever even suspected her. She added that people get caught because they acted guilty. She had no guilt or other emotion. She acted completely normal, didn't sneak or hide, and took what she wanted. She also added that she still does it now and then just to keep in practice.

I asked if she had graduated from high school and she had. When I asked about the ceremony, she said she wouldn't know since she didn't go, and asked why would she want to or care? I asked if she kept in contact with anyone from that time and she actually rolled her eyes at me.

***

Next, I asked what she did after and she answered what and whoever she wanted. Trying to keep her from going sideways, I asked about her work life. She told me that she'd had a bunch of jobs when she was younger. It depended on what she needed or wanted at the time as to who she became when she applied or was interviewed. Her resume was flexible because they rarely checked it. Her strength was her person-to-person skills. With her ability to read a person or situation easily, she could craft the process however she needed to. She said if she got an interview, she always got the job. As a conclusion, she told me that when she passed her mid-twenties, she began working for herself. It was easier. Because she moved so much, she could just take it with her and adapt it somewhere else instead of starting over with all the other every time.

I asked her where she had lived, and she said that she had taken the time to write it down once and it had been forty-three places but added there had been about five more added since that time. I asked why so much, and she said it was for different reasons. Whether it was a relationship or just because she wanted to, it was pretty great. I've lived a lot of different places, but I said it sounded tiring and she said it was actually exciting. She explained that when you never stayed in one place, no one ever got to see the real you and she could start over, sometimes playing the same games or sometimes creating new ones. It was situational and again, depended on what she needed or wanted.

I then moved onto criminal enterprise and bad habits. She smoked cigarettes once in a while, usually in character, but I knew that. Anything else? She said that she had never done any of that because she liked to be clear-headed, and sometimes had to be, to work whatever it was at the time. She also added that in a pinch she could fake it and that worked too. She gave an example of being in a bar and someone buying her a drink. She wouldn't drink it but if they were distracted or went to the bathroom or whatever, she would give it to someone and say they had bought her the wrong one. That way she made the person she was playing happy and usually met a new person or two for later. As far as crime, she had told me about the shoplifting, but what else? She said it depended on your perspective if any other things she had done were actual crimes or just cruel, but we could talk about that later when different conversations came up if I wanted.

I moved on from that and into relationships. She said not counting youthful indiscretions, one night and no night stands, or quick plays for quick results, that, in some way, she had used every one of them except the first one. Before I could ask about that person, she kept me off of it by saying that fat girls were the easiest and whenever she really needed something quickly, she would go out and find one. It never took long.

With a deep breath, I had to ask what she had done without going into too much detail. She said that the first time she actively pursued a fat girl was in her mid-twenties.

***

Before I continue, I should describe her so you can picture how she can do these things so easily and carelessly. She is very good-looking. I'm sure she knows it. She is slender and fit and takes care of herself. She has a good body for clothes, which is why she can change that around so easily. She is taller for a woman, around five-nine, or five-ten. She has jet blue eyes and jet-black hair. I guess if you didn't know her, you would think she was sexy. She moves like a cat and has that mysterious sensuality that attracts others like forbidden fruit. She speaks well, is confident, considerate, and well-mannered.

***

But, back to where I was. She went a little sideways and said that not only are they fat, but many have low self-esteem, for which she was grateful, and that those women would fall for just about anything. She said that she always found one really good trait and focused on that and tried not to look at the rest. Although she gave me actual examples, I won't share those since they are basically cruel. But she told me that she could work them for cars, a place to live, or anything else she wanted. She said that she had worked someone anywhere from a couple of weeks to two different women for about a year and a half. She thought it was funny that they were clueless the entire time. With a frilly voice, she says, "They were in Love!" She said in those cases, she couldn't help herself because they were so stupid, that as she was leaving, she told both of them exactly what she had done to them and why.

I had to get off that or she'd go sideways again, so I asked about real relationships, or real for her anyway. She said dismissing the first and last, the rest didn't really count. I didn't even bother to ask why. I knew. I focused on the other two instead. They were actually her longest and shortest, but they meant something to her. She said that she had true feeling for both of them and although she probably used the second some, that they were a lot alike and she had probably been used a little too, so it was okay. She said that showed she could have a real emotion and then asked if we could move on to something else.

I decided to stay on a parallel path and asked her if there was anyone or anything that she truly cared about or loved. Without hesitation, she said, "Animals." She loves them and always has. She said they knew that she only cared about what was best for them and didn't care who or what she was otherwise. She has had pets since the day she was born and can't imagine her life without them in it. They are her balance, her companionship, and the one stable influence in her life. I guess I was surprised. Though with her, I shouldn't be.

I moved to hate then. With no prompting, she said she hates bullies and mean people. She went on a bit of a rant and said that if you're a bully, you really are a loser. And that you know it. Which is why you're a bully. She said that bullies push people around that they can easily dominate or that won't fight back. She said they lacked confidence in general but often specifically about physical shortcomings and then overcompensated for them by taking it out on others. She said they often grew up to then beat their wives, kids, and probably kicked their dogs too. She said the way they tried to make others feel is how they actually felt about themselves. She told me then that she scared people like that. And did it on purpose. She then said that mean people are just as bad as bullies. They're mean for the same reason, because they lack confidence. They think if they're mean to you maybe you won't see the scared little person behind it. They'll just scare you off instead. If they lash out at anyone and everyone, at any situation, you won't realize they don't like themselves much either.

It is obviously a subject she is passionate about. In its way, I got to see her with a true emotion. She told me that she could tell that I didn't understand how she could be a champion for some and use the rest and finished by saying that she would always stand up for those who couldn't. We sat for quite a while after that outburst and talked about her views on protecting those that need it. She said she would never target someone in that position. They already had enough going on. She added that she rarely targeted any minority for the same reason.

***

At what was to be our last meeting, I started out with a softball. Or so I thought. I asked her what she had been up to lately. She smiled huge. She said over the last few months, she had been gaslighting somebody and it was so much fun.

She told me who, why, and different actions she had taken to accelerate the situation, but I will definitely not share any of it here.

I asked if she had been doing anything else. She said she had been feeling like it was time to move on and that always makes her antsy. She went on the road for a while recently but that didn't help since she came back here. She said she had one more trip to make and if she liked it, she was just going to stay. She said in the last year or so, to reduce stress, besides the gaslighting, she had caused one person to lose their job, one to get demoted, and one to get evicted. I just shook my head.

With trepidation, I opened my mouth again anyway and asked if there was anything she'd like to add. She nodded and said that she had agreed to talk to me so people could understand that people like her aren't as evil and/or bad as they are often portrayed. She went on to say, "The truth is that I'm not really all bad. I'd say about fifty to sixty percent of the time, that I'm a regular person. I just have a cut-off switch that you don't. I may be sociopathic. I've always understood the way I saw, did and felt things was very different from regular people. I started researching myself when I was young and first started noticing. I think you have to know yourself. I have also gotten off track. My point was that no matter who or what I am, I love the world. I think that it's pretty cool overall. Of course, that's dismissing the eighty percent of the people in it that just blindly go along every day. Those types I can't tolerate at all and are also usually the type I target. But the rest are all right."

***

I think that says it all.

My Thoughts and Views

I haven't shared close to all of the examples or people of the stories she shared. I have a head full of the people that she's used along her path. From her perspective, I honestly think most had no clue they had been. Unless she wanted them to find out. That is the cruel side of her. She is outwardly like many around her. As long as you don't look into her eyes.

I watched her talk about shoplifting and crimes while in the next sentence discussing, in depth, psychology and eastern philosophy. I listened to her talk about her enjoyment of lying while at the same time being brutally honest. In situations like this I really do ponder the nature versus nurture debate. In her case, I believe that she always was the way she is but that it was amplified by her early life and her intelligence.

My overall assessment is that she is personable, intelligent, and charismatic. I talked to her for two weeks and have shared only a very little bit of what we spoke about. She really can be anyone she chooses to be. I think I got to see many of the sides. She is complicated. She is truthful in her lies. She is usually amused with the world and with herself, though she can also be deadly serious. That was the scarier part to me. She is most definitely a sociopath. Not one single doubt about that.

The Fruit Picker

SW Florida. In town to run errands, he stopped at the dealership to get his car tuned. Since it would be a while, he looked up the bus schedule to find out how to get downtown. I met him when he sat down beside me. We were riding the 12.

***

Born and raised in west central Florida, he grew up playing in his family's orange groves then working them alongside his father. Now they are his. But he never wanted that life. He had more in mind for himself. None of those things involved staying where he grew up. Don't get him wrong. He loves his family and enjoyed his early years, but even back then he understood he wasn't like the people around him. After his father died, too early, he felt an obligation to stay on.

He is quietly unhappy. The grove does well. He is a fair boss. And it is hard work. But he sees himself as an intellectual laborer or a philosophical farmer. His house is filled with books. He told me that he is a gay man in a foreign land.

I had him tell me about having an orange farm or grove. Growing up in North Carolina, I only knew tobacco and more standard crops. After about twenty minutes, it was apparent that although he didn't want to be there, he knew what he was doing. We laughed as he told me about having rotten orange snowball fights as a kid. I told him we had done the same, but with pine cones. And the green ones really hurt.

At that point, we started talking about his secret life. He corrected me and said it wasn't a secret with family and close friends, it just wasn't really talked about.

As a gay person, I talked to him for quite a while about my thoughts and views on being gay, what it meant, and how to live your life. The main point I was trying to share was that if someone was really your friend and/or really cared about what was best for you that they would support and encourage you to be who you were. He told me that at this point it was as much him as them and that they had all just gotten comfortable with the way things were. I said that comfortable was another word for safe and it was another way to not have to put yourself out there and deal with what would happen when you did.

I asked him then if he was happy. He thought for a minute then answered, no. Like we had talked about, he is very good at what he does but he doesn't want to be doing it.

In his personal life, he loves his family. But at the same time, he doesn't really have a personal life. I asked about that and he actually blushed. I laughed and said, "Well?" He explained that he was probably the stereotypical gay country boy. That he took trips to Key West, Miami, Orlando, and he had been to Atlanta, Washington, and a few others. He had also been on a couple of gay cruises. I asked if that was enough for him and he said that it wasn't. He told me that over the years he had met a couple of guys that he really liked but after the vacation was over, they only communicated by email and sometimes phone and that was really no way to make an adult relationship. I then asked him if he had ever had a sustained relationship and he said that he hadn't. Then he added that he thought it was too late. I told him I was going to kick his butt if he didn't straighten up. He laughed.

***

Our next meeting was on National Coming Out Day. I started us out by apologizing for preaching at him and told him that wasn't my way, but I felt like a protective older sister or something. He laughed and said that he needed one. Back to the gay, I asked him what he was doing for our day and he said nothing. I pushed again and said to try it. Start small and just pick one person that he thought well of and tell them. He said he would think about it, which usually means no.

I switched to something more comfortable for him and asked what he really wanted to do. He said that if he had his choice, I told him he did, that he wanted to teach at a small college. I asked him what he would do. He said he would like to teach Sociology and that he really wanted to cover so much but he wanted to focus on southern peoples, the different groups, and how they came to be who and what they are. He added that he thought that of all the regions, there were probably more misconceptions about southerners. I said that if he was committed to the farm, that he should start a blog and possibly a website with the blog on it. I went on to say he could build a good one for about fifteen dollars a month. We spent the rest of our time being nerds together and I told him that if he brought his laptop the next time, I could show him some different things.

***

Sunday morning, I got there first. Back at our favorite convenience store for push button coffee, he walked up with his laptop under his arm and a big smile on his face. He sat down, and with no preamble, said, "I did it." I asked him what he had done. He told me that he took my advice, I laughed, and he smiled and continued on. He had told the pastor of his church. I said, "And?" He smiled bigger and said that although he felt this amazing weight lifted, that in reality it was no big thing. There was no reaction other than kind words and acknowledgement of what he had accomplished. I told him that was awesome, and he agreed. Then he went on to say that he was going to work to be more open because he liked the way it felt. I told him that he was empowering himself and added that it had to feel great.

To give him a break, I told him to get his laptop cranked up. Once he had, I started showing him different sites and we talked about how to promote, how to get attention, how to engage people, and how to get them to come back. I told him that Sociology was fine and interesting, but it had to be readable and understandable. It had to engage. I told him that for me personally, my goal was to make people think. We talked about that for a while. Next, I told him to remember that it wasn't a school, so he had to be willing to add his thoughts and feelings to what he was writing about and why it was important to him. After we had talked about all of his options, I had him flip to my blog. He seemed to like that quite a bit. I told him that he could follow me and when he had his up, I would do the same. Once again, we spent the rest of our time happily ensconced in Nerdville.

***

Before our next scheduled meeting, he contacted me to change it. He said he had some things to get done. No worries I told him, we rescheduled for a week later.

On the day, he walked in and he looked different somehow. I told him so. He plopped down and said, "I guess so. It's all your fault anyway." I laughed and told him that often throughout my life that was the case and then asked what I had done this time. He looked at me seriously and said, "You've changed my life." I told him thanks but probably not and that any change had come from inside him. He rolled his eyes and said, "Fine. You motivated me to change mine then." When I asked about what, he began talking and I sat impressed as I listened for about thirty minutes as he shared what he had started.

The first thing he did was have a family meeting. He said it lasted well into the evening as they talked about most everything. The conclusions were that his siblings were going to step up and be more active in the groves. It was a family business, and everyone had become comfortable and complacent with the way things were. He told them that for twenty-two years he had pushed his own wants and needs aside to be the responsible one and that it was time for the others to do their part. I asked him about hurt feelings and he said that at first they all seemed defensive but that after all the hours of talking they were doing okay. I next asked him how he felt about it all. He said that it had taken him about three days to get up the nerve but once he had, he was a little scared and nervous, but also excited.

I asked him what else was going on. He laughed and said he was going to work on getting a personal life. Then he blushed. I laughed. He continued that he was going to continue to put himself out there because he liked the way it felt. I said, "Good for you," and then asked if he had a plan. He answered, "Not really. I guess I'll just figure it out as I go." I laughed again.

Next was his career. He would still be involved with the grove, it was a part of him now, but he would be taking much more time for his joy. He had some thoughts in his head and was going to try his hand at writing a book. I told him that was awesome. I added that if he was still thinking about the blog and if he was, that he needed to connect those through there and start getting his name and brand out there and into people's heads. He said that he had started building the site and sketched out his first blog. He pulled some papers out of his pocket and handed them to me. When I opened it, I looked up at him and he said, "Read it. Please?" I sat quietly and did just that.

The writing was good. What he was trying to convey was clear, but I told him that he was hiding behind his words and needed to try and interject more of himself. I shared that throughout my life, people could tell that I enjoyed what I did and believed in it and that often made the difference.

He also told me that he was looking into community colleges or continuing education programs to start out on his quest to teach. He felt rusty and nervous and he thought that the atmosphere of either would be his best bet. He went on to tell me that he had been researching to find out what he needed to do and who was looking for what he was offering. I told him he was making me tired just listening, so he must have worn himself out. He surely covered a lot and had been focused and working hard. He agreed that indeed he was, but he felt a sense of happiness and accomplishment that he hadn't in a long time. At the end of our time together, he asked if we could meet one more time. I told him we most definitely could.

***

For what was to be our final meeting, once again I beat him to our spot. I was drinking my coffee when he walked in, looking serious with a messenger bag over his shoulder. He got his coffee then joined me.

Once again, his first comment was, "I did it." I laughed and asked him what he had done this time. He answered, "Most everything we talked about." I told him if that was the case, he had definitely been busy and then I commented that the oranges must be taking care of themselves. He told me that his family had been doing a lot of the work while he worked on his own stuff, which was awesome.

I said, "Okay, big guy, show me. Come on. Let's see." He smiled, opened his bag, and started pulling out all kinds of folders and his laptop. He asked me what order and I shrugged. He opened the first folder and showed me his resume. It looked sharp and I told him so. He said he had a headache because he started researching continuing education and community colleges in his area and was both pleased, somewhat saddened, and excited that there was such a huge need for educators in those areas in central Florida. He picked the seven he liked the best and sent off all his stuff. He had already been contacted by three of them. I asked him how he felt about all that and he said, "Nervous." I smiled. He's such an engaging guy that he'll do fine and they'd each be lucky to have him. I told him the same. He went on to say that he would probably start with continuing education because that was in the evening and he would still be involved with the grove. I agreed with his thoughts on that.

He got out his computer next. I got my first shock as he pulled up an online dating service. He had signed up. It was so cute and he blushed again. It was a great picture and I asked him who took it. He said, "My sister. She helped me with all this. I think she's going to stick her nose in and help me pick people to contact." I laughed and told him that was really cool. "It is. She's like me with that. Once she makes up her mind, she jumps in with both feet. I think she's more excited than I am." We talked about his new and budding social life and he blushed again. That's one of my favorite things of him. He still has that capability. It's kind of charming, really.

Next, he pulled up the beginnings of what his new website would look like. That looked sharp too and I told him so. He had done really well with it. He pulled out the same blog writing that he had done before, and he had really ramped it up and interjected himself into it. It had the depth that it had lacked and was nicely done. He looked at me then. "I took your advice with that. Do you really like it? Or are you just saying that?" I asked him if I looked like that type and he laughed and said, "No. I can't say that you do." "Right?"

We ended up sitting and talking for over an hour about everything and nothing. When it was time to go, he asked if he could hug me. He most definitely could. I thanked him for being a part of what I was doing, and he mumbled and stumbled and said, "I wasn't sure at first, but I'm glad I made myself do it. I've learned a lot about myself, just over the last month. Thank you. For everything." I told him he was very welcome. I had enjoyed getting to know him as well. He waved over his shoulder as he was leaving.

My Thoughts and Views

He's a guy you just really can't help but like. His kindness and genuineness are not put on. Not at all. That's just who he is. I'm sure most anybody that is in his life are glad that they are. It was a gift to meet and talk with him.

As far as his life. Well, that's easy. In his quiet and gentle way, he is going to kick butt. Like he said about his sister, he is jumping in with both feet. You can see it. He is confident enough that once he does, he is committed to seeing it through. He's going to be a very good teacher. He's not a voice-raiser, arguer. He shares. Wherever he ends up with that, I can see him being on his students' favorite teacher list.

As mentioned, I think the sweetest thing about him is his ability to blush. It's truly cute and also shows the type person he is. Although he often kept parts of him to himself, it wasn't his goodness. With his decision now to no longer hide any part, that will be a gift both for him and those he comes in contact with in whatever context. All I can say is, "Watch out world. Here he comes."

The Killer Smile

Mississippi. I actually met him through his sister. We struck up a conversation while waiting for the bus to go downtown. She talked more about her brother than herself and she told me that if I wanted a really interesting story, that I should meet him. She agreed to take me to do that.

***

I met him at (or in) the jail. The first thing I noticed when we met is his teardrop tattoo by his left eye. He is now awaiting trial for murder. As his sister introduced us and I sat down, we had a stare-off to start our interview. I think it was a tie. She then went back to the waiting room to visit him after we were done.

***

He was born into the Cabrini-Green high-rise projects of Chicago. For a visual reference, they were the ones used as the backdrop for the TV show Good Times.

Born to a single mother, he was one of three. His brother and sister were unsure of their parentage and so was he. His mother told them all it could have been a few different people. She didn't care, and after a while, neither did he.

There were few family examples of a male authority figure in his world so eventually he sought his own, although he probably didn't realize that's what he was doing at the time.

His mother wasn't a druggie though she'd smoke weed every now and then. She didn't really drink either. He says she was just kind of beat down. She had grown up poor and also hadn't had a lot of good examples. He says that he just remembers her looking tired a lot, like she had mostly given up already.

I asked him to tell me a good memory from his early years and he had to think for a minute. Then he told me that she had worked as a maid in one of the nice downtown hotels and used to bring them little treats when she could. She'd bring things like the candies left at turn-downs, the little packs of Kleenex, sometimes leftover banquet sweets, things like that. He says that he knows it doesn't sound like much but when he was young it showed she thought of them. He equates that small gesture with love. I agreed.

He went to inner city schools and he says that they were just as tough as you'd think, even elementary school. He said he can remember older kids always hanging outside the fence, flashing money, hanging with pretty girls, having nice clothes and shoes. Most of the kids he went to school with were as poor as he was. They wore hand-me-downs, thrift store clothes, and Kmart shoes. It was hard not to look. Everyone knew how they got those things, but you still looked.

***

Looking at him now, you can see the years, he's thirty-eight, but for lack of a better word, he's pretty. He has caramel skin, soulful eyes, and long eyelashes. His hair is braided back in rows. When I told him that, he thanked me but looked embarrassed. When I asked why, he told me that his looks were considered a weak spot with the people that became his crew but that when he was young, they did work in his favor to get him out of trouble with his mom, teachers, and others.

We went back to those years for a bit. He said his mom did try to do what she thought was right. He was in the Boys and Girls Club and other outside activities. He says truthfully there were a lot there that cared. They had started out where he was too, but until about fifth grade, he was shy and didn't stand out. He quietly said that he always knew he felt different but didn't know what it meant or how to express it. He said it so quietly at first, I had to ask him to repeat it. When he did, I asked him when he figured it out and what it was.

He told me in fifth grade he figured out he was gay. He didn't really know the word but had heard it and knew it was him. He always hung around with the girls and he realized he was looking at the boys the same way they were. He added that was more dangerous than his neighborhood and that being a faggot in the 'hood was not something to be proud of or to brag about. He'd already had to front and now he had to do it for two different reasons.

That front lead him to the gangs when he hit junior high. He adds that's when his life started becoming what it was now.

***

It started near the end of fifth grade. He finally started kind of hanging at the fence and talking to the older kids. By the time school was out, they trusted him enough to give him a test drive. With his mom working, they were on their own a lot in the summer. The neighbor ladies kind of kept an eye out but they had their hands full too, so it wasn't hard to get loose as long as he showed his face now and then.

He became a drug runner. It started with a few building to building runs but they'd give him like ten bucks. He was hooked. That was more money than he'd ever had. I asked what he did with it and he laughed and told me that what any eleven-year-old would. He bought food for himself and his brother and sister. He added that never before had a Chicago deep-dish tasted so good.

Through that first summer, he ran and ran. He said his mom had to see new things showing up but never asked. He thinks she was afraid to. By the end of summer, he was officially a baby thug.

He walked into junior high feeling powerful, confident, and strong. He went on to explain that was the real hook. Not the drugs, which even now he's never touched, and he said truthfully, it wasn't even the money. It was the power, the sense of belonging, and the sense of brotherhood.

He also says that he admits there was also a sense of payback for those that had given him a hard time in the past. He then saw a cross between fear, surprise, and respect from those same people. And liked it.

I asked how he did in school. He said that he had always overall been a decent student. He didn't stand out or cause trouble, and he showed up because it was somewhere to be that wasn't home. There was heat in the winter, he always got to eat, and he saw his friends. I asked if anyone had made an impression on him to that point and he said no, that he'd had some okay teachers but none that had inspired him or anything like that.

In junior high, it was much the same, but he was starting to pull away from it as he hung with his crew more and more. He also had the usual teen anger, though it was amplified by his circumstance. He was also fronting most of the time by then. If there was a class or teacher he liked, or if he saw a cute guy, he acted more like a hood to cover.

He and his sister grew closer too. They always had been the closest anyway since they were also closest in age. He said that outlet helped him keep his sanity since he told her everything.

Pressured by peers, he finally had sex with a girl in eighth grade. When I asked about it, he just made a face like a little kid eating broccoli and shook his head. I laughed. I asked him about his secret side and he laughed then. He said that happened not too long after and he knew it was right for him but still a dangerous situation. I asked how he managed, and he said that one of the boys he went through school with was like him and they managed to hook up. Both were terrified. He said once they were "friends like that" they started figuring out ways to sneak off to Chicago's gay area of Boystown without it seeming like that's what they were doing. He said it was only about ten miles away, but a completely different world than his day-to-day.

***

Our second meeting was two days later. Different from our first meeting, I sat down and he smiled. He looks young and still innocent when he does. Of course, he's neither.

After a couple of minutes of light conversation, we started back where we ended. Boystown. I asked him to tell me about his first memory of going there. He said he was underage and no one cared and that he and his friend were like starstruck ghetto rats as they quite literally stood in the middle of the sidewalk and stared. He said it was overwhelming as everywhere he turned there were gay men of every type imaginable and they all seemed really happy about it. There was no hiding, no down low, they were just gay. It was all new to him and he didn't know how to feel about it. He said that he knew they were being looked over and even being cruised some. Both good-looking and fit with that air of danger, they got the white boys excited. He laughed when he said it even though it was true.

He continued that the first night was more like a recon. They stuck together and went in and out of various clubs and bars, were offered drinks, which he declined, and his friend accepted. When they headed back to the hood, he got his thug persona going on again and started home from the subway. When he got there, he woke his sister up and told her all about it.

Back in his world, I asked him if now that he had seen a positive gay world, he had a tougher time with his front. He said not really, he was already very tough, and he just compartmentalized his life or lives.

As far as school went, he still showed up. When his crew gave him crap about it, he let them know that he was being somewhat smart. He wasn't being obvious in his dealing and he was staying under the radar. He said it was really double smart because the war on drugs was going all in at that point. He watched all those that were flashy and ghetto fabulous getting busted then disappearing. He was just a young, black, high school student that happened to live in one of the worst projects in the country.

I asked if he was still enjoying it and he admitted that it was still okay and served multiple purposes in his world. Until eleventh grade. He was, by then, living three lives. Four, if you counted the one at home. The summer between eleventh and twelfth grade, he got arrested. Although it ended up being pled down from a lesser offense to a much lesser one, he now had a record. He had no priors, so he didn't get jail time. Still.

He says that took him fully to the other side and he never went back to school. I told him that was really stupid with only a year left and he said, at that time, he was starting to be stupid. He figured he had a record, no one would ever hire him anyway, what was the point, and all the rest of the self-defeating things he could think of.

He was heavy in the gay scene and heavy in the gang world. He said the pretty boys liked to buy him presents and treat him. It was cool to be hooked up with a thug. He didn't mind. He got a lot of attention, had a lot of fun with many, then back to the hood he would go.

I asked him about his family at that time. He said that by then his mom was a floor supervisor and worked more, his older brother was in the Marines, having gotten the hell away from Chicago, and his sister was honor roll, a cheerleader, and doing great. His face still lit up when he talked about her.

He added that he, on the other hand, was the troublemaker. He was hardly ever there, always ending up somewhere else. He helped his mom with house stuff and she still never asked, but he spoiled his sister rotten and made sure she had any and everything she needed.

But his crew was the focus of his life. The drug business, the enforcement, the crime. He was fearless (or stupid) and to prove himself, would take on all the jobs and things he could tell no one really wanted to. He was arrested again less than a year after that first time. Not only was he a repeat offender now, his charge was bigger. He was also now eighteen. He ended up with a new felony conviction and a year. He served it all in the Cook County Jail, which is still known as one of the worst in the country. He said he learned a lot, and none of it good.

He was early-released after nine months and came home a different person. After celebrating with his crew, the first place he headed was Boystown to release some of the pent-up rage and loss he was feeling. He was surrounded by his people and he remembers it feeling so good.

I asked him about that part of his life while in jail and he said you could have blow

 jobs most anytime, but it was more a power thing than a gay thing since everyone he knew did it. It was kind of like gay for the stay but never spoken of. I told him I had meant companionship and friendship, but he said either was too dangerous and he avoided both.

***

On the other side, he was moving up. He now had his stripes. He had a building reputation as a hard ass, he was feared and respected. He was also making ridiculous amounts of money. I asked what he did with it. He said much of what you'd expect but most was hidden away as a college fund for his sister. She was graduating soon. He smiled huge as he said when that day came, without prejudice, he was the proudest person there as he watched her walk across the stage in the top ten of her class. I asked if she went to college after all that. He said that yes, she had. She had no choice. He laughed and said he would have dragged her there himself. She also went far away as she accepted a partial scholarship to the University of Miami. He added that everything that partial scholarships and grants didn't pay for, he did. He finished by saying that made everything he had done worth it, no matter what.

I cut in for a minute. I asked him if that was how he ended up in Florida, and he said yes, that it was how he made it there. He isn't from Mississippi. This is just where his crimes were committed and where he was arrested and charged.

***

I asked him how many times he had been in jail or prison over the last twenty years. He said he didn't have the number of arrests, but he said it had been around half of those years between little and big stuff. Most were short stints, a year or less, but he did five years for a violent assault. He went to Menard Penitentiary and has quite a few stories about his time there. He said that was about midway through the years. When he got out of there, his sister was grown, she was a college graduate, married, had a cute little girl, and worked for the state. That was when he moved to Florida. She pleaded and pressured him to come and he landed in Miami.

He said where Chicago was in your face, Miami lulled you with the weather and beaches, but was much deadlier. The drug business was huge, there were a lot more hands in it, and instead of being concentrated in the ghetto, it was black, white, Spanish, Caribbean. It was international. It also oozed wealth. He was surprised that the very high-end people didn't even try to hide it. He also said that he disappointed his sister since he knew some people that knew some people and pretty quick, he was right back in the game.

I asked how he had gotten from there to here and he said he was currently incarcerated on the charge of second-degree murder and drug trafficking and would soon stand trial. The state trial would be first for the murder, then the Feds would have their turn on the drug charges. I told him not to talk about any of it to me other than what he just shared because our conversations weren't privileged. He said okay but that it didn't really matter because his life on the outside was over.

***

We took our conversation in another direction. He is an HIV positive man. When I asked him if he knew from who or where, he didn't. He had been surprised when he found out during his medical testing during one of his incarcerations. I asked if he thought he had passed it on to anyone else and he was unsure. To me, that means yes.

We talked about his life and his choices throughout it. He's somewhat retrospective and thoughtful. Of course, he's had many years to think about it. He says that every step in his life led to the next, sometimes wrong steps, but moving him forward and through. He thinks about people he's known. Many are dead, many more in prison, some still doing their thing.

His mom is doing okay. She's got his brother and sister that make sure she does. His brother made the military his career and has seen action two different times. He'll be ready for retirement soon. His sister, well, he says she is amazing. I asked if he ever heard from his original "friend" and he said that, oddly, he does. Every now and then a letter will show up. His sister still keeps the connection, so he always knows where to find him. He said he's doing okay too. Still in Chicago, but not in the projects. He's made a life and is living it.

I asked if he felt he had lived his. He was quiet for a couple of minutes and said that though his choices weren't ones others might make, that for the most part, they were right for him when made. He takes responsibility for all of them. He never deflects or blames, and he is no longer angry.

In the space and place he is in now; he is at peace with it all. His final comment to me was that it was still worth it.

My Thoughts and Views

It may seem contradictory, but he is actually a good person inside. In the world he grew up in, which most can't imagine, he still had the same core beliefs that many do. He has always stood by his friends and always took care of his family. He was respected in his profession, though it was criminal enterprise, and he took responsibility for all his mistakes.

Did he have other options? Sure, he did. Did he know he did? Often, no. He took the cards he was dealt and played his hand the only way he knew how.

As far as his current situation, I don't know the details, though he again takes responsibility for all of his choices. That says a lot about him in any context.

What I do know is that when I looked back at him as I was leaving him for the last time, real tears had joined his tattooed ones.

The Church Lady

SW Florida. We met at the downtown bus depot while we were both waiting for the 5. We had about twenty minutes so we started chatting.

***

She is a true Floridian, born and raised. She comes from a large family with five siblings. She has four of her own and says that each of her siblings have kids too, from two to five. I shook my head as she continued that both her parents did too, her mom had four and her dad, five. I laughed and told her that I didn't even think I knew that many people, let alone had that many relatives. She laughed too and patted my leg. She has a gentle way about her, but you can tell it's over a steel spine. She is one tough cookie.

She told me that both of her parents were stern but good people. "You have to remember how times were then in the south for black people. Not only did we have to follow all the family and church rules, but the rules of a Jim Crow world." She looked up in thought, "I think girls had it a little easier than boys, but no matter, it was no cakewalk for any of us."

We talked about that and I told her I grew up just as desegregation started coming though the Brown decision had been ten years before. I followed and told her that so many of the adults around me thought "they" were so lucky to go to "our" schools. She nodded in understanding and I continued that my parents thought any kind of prejudice or racism was just stupid, to always value a person by who they were, and that we were often the odd ones out relative to social thought. She said that they must have been educated and god-fearing. I laughed and added Yankees and immigrants that had been raised in a different world than the American south.

We completely sidetracked into that world as she told me about learning as a little one, in the early 1950s, where you could and couldn't go, who had separate entrances and seating, who you could look in the eye and who you'd better not, who the good people were and most definitely who the bad were. "You have to understand that one mistake could be a life or death decision." I told her that I couldn't imagine that. That although I knew it was wrong and could and did empathize with every part of all of it, that I was white and could never know that balance of anger, fear, and pride. I shared that growing up gay in the south had some similarities but that in the end, I was still white. I told her about a conversation that my good friend and I had one day. She is black, gay, and southern. As our conversation had ended, she said, "I can hide the gay if I want, but I can never hide the black."

She told me what it was like to go to separate schools. How socially it was safe and nice, you knew everyone, etc., but the books and equipment were the ones the white people didn't want or need anymore, the schools were clean but not well maintained, and continued that she could obviously go on but that her point was, that although you had to fight for it and work twice as hard sometimes, if you wanted to get an education you would. Because the smart ones knew that was the true key to freedom and equality. That the anger was necessary at times, but it had to be balanced with knowledge to work.

To give the serious a break I told her about an experience I had in first grade. I had been in the back of the classroom kissing a boy and we got sent to the principal's office because of it. As I finished that, I told her that even little, he and I both understood it was because he was black and I was white. She laughed and said, "That was humorous and a shame too." I told her it really was but we both knew why and that was good. She asked if I knew what had happened to him. I told her he was still goofy and cute, and doing okay.

Just as we finished, the bus arrived. We sat together and talked a little more. She was getting off before me so we set a time two days later to meet at the downtown library.

At our second meeting, we headed upstairs and found a couple of chairs to sit in. After some light conversation, I asked more about her parents. She talked about her father first. She smiled as she told me that he was the soft touch of the two. "You have to understand his life was so hard. He'd talk now and then about growing up on a poor farm in central Florida during the depression, but he didn't tell us everything, not even close." Her eyes watered a little. "He was a proud man and a strong one, physically and mentally, he had to be. He wasn't educated, he had to work on the farm, but he was smart. He served in World War Two, and as he always said, he won't no stevedore. He served in the Second Cavalry in Europe. He was so proud of that. It's because of that service that my family grew up in a little better circumstances than some." I asked her why and she told me that Harry Truman was one of her father's heroes. Not just for his service but because he never tried to be something that he wasn't. Even though he didn't desegregate the military until 1948, that act also carried over to veterans somewhat and her father was able to obtain a city job that he worked his entire life. That enabled her family to have a sense of security and she knew just how lucky they were. She looked at me and said, "I learned so much from him about perseverance and about thinking things through first. He was a good man."

We moved onto her mother. She smiled. "The strict one. She stayed home, that was the way then. But she was very involved in church activities and dragged all of us right along with her. We grew up in the church as much as we did the home. But she had to be strict with all of us. With all the things you and I have spoken of, it was her mission to ensure we all made it through the minefields safe and whole. Education and religion were our guiding paths and she made sure we towed the line. We didn't even question her. Too scared to. I think she bossed my father too." She laughed at that. "She had some talents though. She could cook, that's for sure. I can remember entire days when she, my aunties, and my grandmother would take over the kitchen. It was a sight and smell to behold. Holidays were the best though." She smiled at the memory and continued, "She could also grow anything. We had a little garden that we always helped with and we had something fresh out of it year around. Her flowers were beautiful too. She had that touch. But her true secret love was that she could paint. They were very good. My sister and I would sneak sometimes and sit quietly on the back porch and watch her. I don't think she ever knew. That's how I like to remember her. Away from motherhood, troubles, responsibilities, and everything else. You could see her joy."

After a break we switched to her siblings and she shared anecdotes about each of them, their personalities, senses of humor, misadventures, and anything else that came up. I could just see the six of them. They were a tight family unit.

She is the oldest and I asked her what they had all grown up to be. "My mother beat college into all of us. She said even if she had to go with us and sit beside us, we were going. That was one of her proudest accomplishments. All six of us graduated college." We talked for a while about how they had managed to do that. We talked about financial aid, extra jobs, family help, etc. It was even more evident that they were a unit. It was a family effort to get each of them through. As the younger ones started, the older ones helped too.

She took a breath and said, "Okay, I was a teacher for forty years. I just retired two years ago." I asked her if she ruled her classroom like her mother had the house. She laughed as she said, "Yes, I did. I did the same to my children too." I smiled and told her that I would have loved it because the ones that had really taught were always my favorites. She nodded and continued, "My sister closest to me still teaches and my baby brother does too. My middle brother made a career of the Army. He is also in the cavalry, family tradition, but now they call it armor. My brother under me is a minister, and my middle sister works for the state." She added that two were close to retirement and the others had some time left.

I asked about her children next. "Two of each. I was a lucky one, no trouble out of any of them. Now, they would act up now and then, but no real trouble." I told her they were scared to. She chuckled. "Like my parents, my husband was the soft touch." She went on to tell me that one daughter had gone to college on a track scholarship. "She could fly, still can. She works with fitness now at a private academy." Her oldest son is a police officer. Her youngest daughter is a teacher, and her youngest son is also career military and also armor. Like with her siblings, we talked for quite a while about the kind of people they were. I could see and hear the pride as she spoke about each of them. When we got on the subject of her grandchildren, she smiled. "I finally get to spoil somebody rotten. Then I send them home." She laughed and laughed as that conversation ended.

We headed back to her experiences in life as a black woman during hard core and overt racism and the laws condoning it, and also as she got older, the beginnings of the Civil Rights and Black Power movements. She said that her church was actually quite active in what Martin Luther King was trying to do and her eyes teared as we spoke at length about the girls in Little Rock, demonstrations, fire hoses, police dogs, voting rights, all rights, and unsolved murders of so many. We spent well over an hour talking in depth about that time. I was very young during that period and just remember snippets of much of it, but she was there and experienced it as a black woman. She told me watching so many die, she often asked herself why, but she understood, from an intellectual standpoint, that they had so others could be free. She looked to the church then to understand and made the parallel that as Jesus had died for so many, all those people, known and unknown, had died for her. She said when Martin Luther King was shot and killed, it was devastating because he had been the face and voice of hope for so many. But like the others before him, his death propelled many that had stayed silent or behind the scenes into action. I told her that I had been five when he was murdered but I remembered it vividly because it was one of those instances that my parents had made me sit and watch so I would always remember what it meant to stand up for something you believe in. She said, mostly to herself, "That's exactly right. Exactly right."

I next asked her to tell me about her church and church activities. She was still going to the one she had grown up in though it was in a different location now. A lot of the congregation were people she had known her entire life and the pastor was a man she had grown up with.

Both of us, not realizing how long we had talked, decided that to talk about that would be an entire interview in itself so we stopped there. She suggested that since I was interested in that part of her life that our next meeting be Sunday at that church. I just smiled. When she asked why, I explained the type of church I had grown up in, my thoughts on it, and then went on to explain that I had begun studying Buddhism in my teens. She just patted my leg and let me know that everyone was welcome and that I'd probably be surprised how much I enjoyed it.

***

At the end of that third meeting, I sat in the park writing out my notes while everything was still fresh. After our morning together, she had been right. I had sat with her and one of her daughters and two of her children. You could tell what it meant to her and how long she had been a part of it. She had primo pew placement. I'd laughed and explained how I had always seen that. She had whispered back that there was probably some truth in it. I also think I met most everyone during our time there. The music was awesome, the pastor was very nice, and the church as a whole was very inviting.

Once I had gotten settled, like I've done my entire life, I just sat back and watched. One thing she may not admit or understand is that she is a very important woman to many.

From much younger to those her own age, I watched as people greeted or spoke to her. It wasn't put on either. It was real. I'd had a little time to walk around and talk to some of them at the break before Sunday School would start. They all spoke well of her and talked about things she had done and continued to do within and for the community.

We left not long after and I asked her if she was going to get in trouble for hooking Sunday School. She laughed, told me I was a mess, and said she was going back after we were done. There is a little playground and park about half a block from the church and we strolled there to sit and talk since the morning was still cool.

The first thing I did was thank her for inviting me and introducing me to so many people. Basically, for sharing her life. She just patted my leg. Again.

I started off asking her about some of the church-based activities that she was involved in. I smiled and said, "Remember, missy. I've talked to people so now I know the truth." She laughed and answered, "How about if I try to list them for you and then if you have any that you'd like to talk more about we can do that?" I told her that was fine. "Let's see. We run a senior program in line with what Meals on Wheels does. We sit and talk with folks and make sure that they eat. We do job assistance and training for various age groups. We do a family wellness program to ensure the young ones having young ones have support, but also the information they need. The pastor does quite a bit of counseling. That's very important as we do have many that really couldn't afford it otherwise. My focus is educational assistance. As you and I spoke before, knowledge is definitely power. For the person and society. That is for any age and involves smaller programs within it. From basic literacy to education for employment purposes. We also work with Adult High School and GED programs. We have a program within that one that begins while a person is still incarcerated. Unfortunately, there is a disproportionate number of young black men in the criminal justice system. We have other programs as well."

When she was done, I told her that I'd like to talk about literacy and education. I shared with her my own background with both of those by volunteering, first, in women's prison, and second, on an Indian reservation. Again, she patted my leg. "I knew you were one of the good ones. That's why I said yes to this."

I thanked her and told her I wanted to be like her when I grew up. She laughed and told me to hush. I went on to tell her that one thing I had noticed in minority communities, whether it be black, gay, Indian, or whatever, was that there was a really high instance of substance abuse and how that had so many implications on not only that person's life and choices, but then continued out from there. She nodded. "The ripple effect. It's both worrisome and sad."

I agreed and shared my experiences through the first years of the Crack Epidemic. I told her about living in Baltimore then and watching as it decimated the entire city and spawned White Flight. I said that although many may have read about it, seeing block after block of abandoned and boarded up rowhouses was devastating. I then talked about how the entire inner city had an air of helplessness. I went on to tell her that my last year there, they had over four-hundred murders. It was terrible to watch happening. It had been like a runaway freight train for about three years and when it stopped, the city looked like a war zone in many areas because it had been.

She was saddened and told me that it had obviously not been that bad here but proportionately, it was just as devastating. She went on to tell me that some days she would feel that same sense of hopelessness as she spoke to one young man after another. "Their anger was palpable. You could feel it and see it. So many seemed to have given up on society because they just assumed it had given up on them, or never cared to begin with." I asked her how she was able to help. She answered, "It sounds simplistic, but just being there. That consistency in word and deed, listening without judging, while at the same time counseling them toward a better way. So many, feeling that anger, were completely reactive to all part of their worlds. We worked very hard to help them to begin to do things for themselves not against who or whatever angered them. We succeeded with so many, but some remained unreachable." She looked at me and said, "Although we are talking about young men, there were adults, women and girls, and even a few older people. But, yes, it was predominantly young men." She shook her head sadly. I asked her if she was still in contact with any of those she had helped. She smiled then. "I am. You even met a couple of them this morning although you didn't know it." I laughed and told her I bet I could pick them out because they would have looked down when they talked to her and said 'yes, ma'am' a lot. She laughed again.

We spoke for about fifteen more minutes about her other programs and then it was time for her to head back to church. As I walked her back, she told me I had to come back now because the people I'd met would be looking for her new friend. I smiled and told her I'd be back for all the church lady potlucks because those definitely rocked it. She laughed as she headed back inside.

We met one more time, but it was more of a wrap up of everything we had talked about with some nice conversation added. I will share that I could talk to her much more. A biography of her life would be a superior read. Maybe in the future, that can happen. I guess we'll see.

My Thoughts and Views

She is an amazing and inspiring woman. Not just to me, that's a given, but I believe to anyone that takes the time to talk to her.

She has so many good traits; Grace, compassion and care being just a few. She is intelligent, kind, and committed. She has her personal faith and has never wavered from her faith in the world as a whole.

In her daily life, she is heroic. In a world that tried at first to limit her, she did not allow it. She steps forward each day carrying all she believes, understands, and has been taught. She walks her path by her own compass.

The people I met all said much the same. They said that when everything around her seems like a storm, she is always the calm in the center of it. As she and I talked about when speaking of her programs, it is her consistency in thought and deed, matched with the person that she is, that makes others look to her.

I like her so much. She is a class act in every way you can imagine. She has, at the very least, my respect and my good thoughts. I, on the other hand, have a new friend. It was a true gift to get to know her.

People I Met (RIP)

The following three are people I have met during my life that made an impact on me for varying reasons. Although none of us met on a bus, all of them deserve for their stories to be told. The place is here. The time is now.

The Statistic

Street smart, tough, a thug, a bad ass. A good-looking, funny, nice guy that's had a very hard life.

***

Born to a fourteen-year old drug addict and raised in a project high rise, his world view was nonexistent, his day-to-day was uncertain at best. He found his definition on the street and found love only from his grandmother.

I met him when he came to interview for a dishwashing position. In my first life as a chef, I always gave people with the right personality and attitude a chance. Although history was considered, it was in the past, not the present.

He was honest about his and he was funny as hell. I hired him with the caveat, "You know I'm going to work your ass off, right?"

He told me later that his first night, he hated me. I had given him a long list of things that needed to be done. He was on his knees, under a prep table, and pulling all the pots and pans out so he could clean it. He was grumbling and bitching about me the entire time. It was pretty funny. He said that he remembered being shaken from his reverie and looking to his right to see me in the exact same position. I smiled and winked. Never ask anybody to do anything you're not willing to do yourself. From that day forward, our friendship grew.

***

From the beginning, he thought he was doomed to become a statistic. As mentioned, his mother was a drug addict on public assistance and living in the projects of Baltimore when he was born. She couldn't take care of herself, let alone a baby, but she needed those checks to buy more drugs. He said that if it wasn't for his grandmother, he probably wouldn't have made it to five. Sometimes he wasn't sure how he had anyway.

Basically, he grew up on the streets. His first view was of chain link. It was put over the stairwells and other openings so no one would jump, fall or be pushed out. Those same stairwells fostered every illegal activity you could imagine and just as many that you really couldn't. But they were also the playground for the little ones. He grew up playing games around the dealers and prostitutes. Although that was dangerous, it was safer than outside, which had become a shooting gallery many days.

By ten he was a drug runner. The dealers liked to use kids under fourteen because even if they got caught, nothing would happen to them in an overloaded juvenile justice system. Plus, he was fast.

By fourteen, he no longer went to school. Nobody but his grandmother cared if he did or didn't. He became a baby thug. Good-looking, agile, funny and not stupid, he could deflect attitude and anger while still getting things done.

He laughed when he said by eighteen, he was ghetto-fabulous. He was doing well in his world. He had the bling, he had the girls, and he'd earned his stripes. He was officially a thug. In his first eighteen years, he had never been out of Baltimore.

By twenty-one, he had a record and had been shot three times. His abdominal scars were wicked. He was such a paradox. I often wondered if he knew. He was very good-looking, model level, he had beautiful eyes, a great body (he laughed and said he got it running from the cops), he was engaging, street smart and truly funny. At the same time, he was a gun-toting, drug dealing, bad ass motherfucker. He also became a baby daddy in his twenty-first year. Or as he told me, one statistic making another.

Not long after his introduction to fatherhood, he went to prison. That was the first time he ever left Baltimore. He said prison changed him, but not for the better. Whereas he thought he was a bad ass, he learned quickly that he wasn't. He was just a punk. His grandmother was the only one that came to see him, but he said he felt like he could see the disappointment in her eyes. Deep down, he was disappointed too. To stay out of the line of fire as much as anything, he got his GED while inside. He wasn't sure why.

After two years, he was a free man. But he said that he felt like the world that he returned to wasn't one he belonged in. He started smoking what he used to sell. Then he was really lost.

The next year of his life, he barely remembers. He was dealing again, but now to cover his own. He slept wherever and got another girl pregnant too. I asked if he'd ever heard of condoms.

He went back inside, jail this time, for simple possession. He was there when his second daughter was born. He told me that if he hadn't been arrested, he would probably have died during that first year out. Somewhere inside, he would fight for himself when stilled and this time he went through drug rehab and job training. When he got out, his grandmother took him in. We met not long after, when he applied for the job. He was twenty-four. I was twenty-five.

***

There was no big production, like we're going to be friends now, we just were. I liked him so much and we were often ridiculous together.

Not long after we met, I took him home with me to meet my girlfriend at the time. She was a bit stuffy and moderately cranky. She was one of those people that insisted on using her full name. I won't use her real one but as an example, if her name had been Catherine, no one would dare call her Cathy. But he did. It was so funny and so cute. You couldn't help but like him. He picked on her, acted silly and called her (Cathy). She just laughed and let him do and say whatever he wanted. He brought out her deeply-buried fun side and truly, that was a gift. Most never saw it and I doubt she remembered she had one. It was love at first site for the two of them though. Sidetracking some, I remember that first holiday party watching as the two of them danced the night away. He showed her joy.

Not too long after that first meeting, I got to meet his grandmother. He called her Mommy because, really, she had been the only constant in his life. She was such a good woman. Almost serene, but she had a steel rod in her back. She was determined not to lose another to the streets as she had lost her daughter. It's funny, grandmother makes her sound old, but when I met her, she was about the age I am now. I liked her so much. When she took him in, she also took his girls. She told me as long as she was alive, there would be no foolishness with the babies. Like their dad, they were both lookers and his oldest daughter looked just like him. I told him it was payback for his earlier behavior.

Over time, I spent many days sitting at her kitchen table and talking while he learned how to be a father. She wouldn't allow any bull. All of them were there so when he wasn't working, those girls were his focus.

***

A couple of months after he started working with me, I told him I was giving him a Saturday off, but he had to spend it with me. My girlfriend and I picked him up very early that morning and headed to Washington for the day. Although only about forty miles away, he had never been there. We had so much fun. We dragged him to every museum we could as well as all the monuments. He fell in love with the Smithsonian and we didn't come near seeing all of it. We sat on the steps of the Lincoln Memorial and munched as we watched the sea of people go by. He was so quiet and for once I didn't pick because I understood why. We stayed the entire day and he fell asleep in the back seat on the way home. I looked at my girlfriend and she had tears in her eyes.

After that, once a month we had an excursion day. I dragged him everywhere you could get to in a day. We went to Philadelphia, western Maryland, the mountains of Virginia, I took him to auctions, historic sites, everywhere. I loved seeing things through his eyes. The excitement and adventure were palpable. I loved him so much.

***

Then his mother died. Although their relationship was a mess, it was like at that point, every feeling he had, came out. He was so hurt. He started calling in sick, which he had never done, and I went and talked to his grandmother. She told me he was confused, sad, angry and a bunch of other things too. He became distant and unreliable.

Then the phone call came.

It was early on a Saturday morning, our date day, and I got a call from a local psych hospital. He had been coherent enough to give them my name and number. They told me he had been brought there from the hospital after he slit both his wrists. He was twenty-six.

I was up and gone so fast. When I got there, I spoke to the nurses for quite a while and then they took me to him. He looked so damn young as he held on to me. He kept apologizing and crying. He couldn't stop. I did too. I could feel every bit of his terror and pain. It was terrible.

I stayed a lot of that first day and he eventually told me what happened. He had been so angry and was somewhat despondent too. He found a crack house, not hard to do, in east Baltimore. He remembered paying for the spot and the drugs and remembers smoking it too. He got up at some point and went in the bathroom. He was so mad at and disappointed with himself. He was no better than her and never would be. He had a straight razor in his pocket and he slit both his wrists.

He should have died, but a crackhead with a heart saved him. When she saw blood coming from under the door, she yelled out, everyone scattered, but she stopped at a pay phone, called 911, gave the address, and said someone was dying. Then she hung up. He never knew who it was.

He stayed in the psych hospital for a month and I spent at least two days a week with him. After that they moved him to a rehab or transition center. There was group and individual counseling, etc. It was to help him re-enter the world. He looked terrified and asked if I'd come to the individual counseling with him. I told him as long as they said okay, I wouldn't be anywhere else. His grandmother had started coming out to visit while he was there, but he said he couldn't even look her in the eye because he felt like a failure. She and I talked a lot and I would go check on her and the girls to make sure they were okay through all those months.

When it was time to leave, he was coming home with me for a while so he could just be. He would get so scared some nights that he would crawl in bed with us. I'd take him for drives to places he liked, and I had my motorcycle then, so he and I would get on it and just go fast so he could scream in the wind. His grandmother and the girls came for Thanksgiving and I took him there for Christmas.

At the beginning of the year, he went home. I had him working part time by then to give him structure and outside focus. He was still somewhat unsteady but doing okay.

***

By March, he was gone again. I couldn't find him anywhere and neither could his grandmother. In May, a couple of weeks before my birthday, she called to tell me that she had found him. I wanted to be excited, but her voice gave her away. He was dead at twenty-seven. Another young black man lost to the streets of Baltimore. He had become the statistic that he always said he was.

Goddamn it.

My Thoughts and Views

I still have such a hard time talking about him. As I sat down to write this, I was doing okay but when it came time to type it out, I had to get up and go walk around the block then come back to it.

We were the couple that made no sense to anyone but us. We loved each other. It was that simple. The white, over-educated, gay young woman raised in a snotty world and the baby-faced, under-educated black young man, raised by the streets. For that two-and-a-half-year period of our lives, we were inseparable. He was such a good person. He was so sweet, so funny, and so smart. But he was often scared to be that person. Even though he could front with the best of them, he was often under-confident in anything outside his comfort zone of the hard world of the streets. There, he understood his place. The rest usually seemed foreign to him. Over the time we spent together we talked about everything, both big and small. I often wished he could see the person I could. I was crushed when he died, and I was mad at him for leaving me and I was mad at him for giving up on himself. I love him still.

***

It's been twenty-seven years since he died, the age he was when he did, and my eyes still tear when I talk about him. I think they always will.

<u>The Streetwalker</u>

If you didn't know him, you would have seen a poor black man with no job and a falling down house. You would have seen him walking the poorest neighborhood in the city at all hours of the day and night. But I don't think he ever gave a thought to what others thought or saw. He was just who he was, walking his own path by his own beliefs.

***

He grew up in Virginia. He grew up in the black part of town. And in his early years, he grew up in a segregated world. Separate schools; separate everything. His parents were both hard-working and well-thought-of. They were among the founders of the small church the family attended. He had four brothers and sisters. Over time, I had a chance to meet them all. He was the next to the youngest.

He was always a good kid, happy-go-lucky with an infectious smile and a sunny outlook. Life was often hard enough. Why add? People all thought well of him. He went through school, graduated, spent three years in the military, then came back to the home he knew.

***

When I met him, I was sure I wasn't going to like him. At all. We met each other through one of the great loves of my life, Mimi dog.

Anyone that truly knows me, knows that I like animals better than people. I lived in the neighborhood he had grown up in and still lived in. At the time I was there, it was completely decimated. The crack epidemic killed it. A lot of the parents had passed on by then and their kids were given the houses. When I say kids, I mean people in their thirties and forties. Many of those same kids were caught up in the horrible nightmare that was crack. Needless to say, many homes were gutted. They were pulling their own pipes out of the walls to sell the copper to buy drugs. There were entire blocks of boarded up and abandoned houses throughout much of the neighborhood. You could purchase a nice Victorian in the bad part, which is where I lived, for five thousand dollars. There weren't many takers.

Anyway, there was this very sexy dog. He was a god-knows-what mix. Probably some Lab, Pit, and a bunch of others. I fell in love immediately. He was obviously the king of the hill though. I called him medium dog because that's what he was. As we moved closer, it just became Mimi dog. I'd see him meandering with a gang following along. Every once in a while, he had scrapes and cuts too. Defending his turf, no doubt. I assumed he was homeless. He wouldn't come near you, was undernourished, had ticks, etc. Whenever I saw him, I would go out and sit on the curb and talk to him. His tail would wag as he stood about ten feet away. I'd throw food his way and he'd eat it while still keeping his distance. I finally got him to come with a pack of hotdogs. He liked those a lot.

Once he did, we were besties. I had a four-foot chain link around the little front yard off the sidewalk. I had an old chair on the porch. It got so whenever he wanted, he would just jump the fence, and he also started sleeping in the chair every night.

One morning I came out and he was covered with blood, beat to hell, and mostly unconscious. Somehow, he had made it over the fence and dragged to the porch. I only had Neosporin and washcloths. I went and grabbed everything then sat on the porch and cleaned him. After, I filled all the holes with the ointment. He just let out a deep breath and closed his eyes. I had my own dogs so he couldn't come in. It was winter and cold. I made what I called a pup tent out of a quilt, turned the chair with the back facing out, and picked him up and put him in it. For days, I would come out in the morning, clean him up, medicate him, shake out the blankets, get him to try to drink a little water, and worry. I also checked on him many times during the day and right before I went to bed each night. About the sixth day, I came out in the morning and his eyes were open and he was wagging his tail. I was in love.

A couple of weeks later I was outside doing something or another and I hear, "Excuse me. Hey, excuse me. I want to thank you." I turned to the voice and saw that beautiful smile. He was in mechanic's coveralls, walking up the street toward me with his hand out. When he made it, he shook my hand, "I've been trying to catch you. Jimmy told me what you did. Thank you so much for taking care of Cujo." I smiled back; you couldn't help it. "Who is Cujo?" Just then Mimi dog came running up to love on me. "That's Cujo." I laughed. "Not to me. That's Mimi dog." He just laughed, then got serious. "I really do want to thank you. I don't know what to say." "You don't have to say anything. Because of you, I met my new boyfriend." He just smiled and laughed.

From that day forward, we were just buddies. I can't even verbalize the person that he was. His attitude lit up everyone that he came in contact with. This is also when I began learning his story and meeting many of the people he knew, as well as his family.

***

After the Navy, he worked for a larger bank as security. Same as everywhere else, his energy made everyone smile. He really liked what he did, and they liked him.

By then, crack had come. He would take a nap until dark after he got home from work, then he would spend the night walking the streets of the neighborhood. He knew the dealers, the crackheads, the old folks, the store owners, He knew them all. He would walk those streets, night after night, making sure the crazy wasn't too crazy. He would call them out too. Letting the hoods know that he knew their mamas, grandmas, aunties, etc., and that he was going to let them know what they were doing. It was his neighborhood and it meant something to him. So did the people in it.

Most merchants and stores had not only left the neighborhood but run from it. In our section, one had stayed. Mr. Kim. He knew him too. One night when he came to do his check-in, he walked in on a robbery. He knew the kid. He was seventeen, strung out, and trying to get money for more. He talked to him, trying to get him to walk away, think about what he was doing, and just stop. The kid shot him five times.

There isn't a reason in hell that he should have lived but he did. Mr. Kim was so grateful. He became like a son to him. He was in the hospital for about five months. It really was that bad. A couple of months later, when the time for the trial came, he went and testified for the kid. He told the judge that it was the drug not the kid. That he knew he was from a good family and made a mistake. He asked that he not be considered an adult. That if he had a chance now, he would make it. That if he went in the system as an adult, they were looking at a lifetime offender. The judge agreed. This is the kind of person he was.

As an aside to that, during his time in jail, the kid got back in school and got his GED. When he got out, he headed to community college. He invited my friend to his graduation because he knew that he had saved his life. He moved forward and became a part of the community. He always looked for the best. Because he did, that's what he often found.

***

That day we met was about three years after. Over time, I got to know most everything about him. He lived behind me and on the other side of the street, about a hundred feet away. The first time I went in his house was because he needed money to eat and had some older things that he wanted me to look at and see if they were worth trying to sell. I was saddened. It was terrible. He had the entire upstairs boarded up and closed off. He had the kitchen blanketed off from the rest of the downstairs, and he had a cot in the kitchen. He had no heat. He was using the gas stove to stay warm.

The house he lived in was the old family home. It seemed to fall apart a little more every day. His parents lived in the good part of the neighborhood by then and let him live there. It used to really bother me because, in reality, his family didn't help him at all other than letting him live in a house with the porch falling off the second floor. He flipped that too. He loved his family and always said that at least he had a roof.

He had one brother, the oldest, that was somewhat of a showboat. He drove and old El Dorado Cadillac. That was a seriously sweet ride. I'd watch him as he'd drop by, bringing this woman and that. I couldn't figure out what the point to his visits were, other than to strut.

My friend had a girlfriend in the years before he got shot. They weren't together anymore but it was obvious that she was a good person and cared about him still. I liked her very much. I met her because she would drop by every couple of weeks, check on him, and make sure he was doing okay. She was the only one in his inner circle that ever did.

I met his parents one Easter. I was invited to come to their church after the services and enjoy a potluck in their fellowship hall. I smiled when I met his dad. He looked just like him. His mother was a very serene woman and I had a feeling that she is where he gained his outlook and attitude. After that day, I would see them out and about, and always stop and chat for a few minutes.

I met his sisters and other brother that Easter as well. As he said, one of his sisters was filled with church. You really couldn't even have a conversation with her. The other was a lot like him. They were only about a year and a half apart, close in temperament and personality.

His other brother was ridiculous. He was the baby and had obviously always gotten away with most anything. Still spoiled, he had a nice smile of his own and a baby face. He was really funny too.

Over time, getting to know them as well as others from his life, I could understand how he became the person that he was. It was the perfect balance of character, personality, and outlook. He had absorbed the good while not falling into the bad.

***

We were each other's holiday date from that Easter on. The first Christmas he came for dinner, he cleaned up and wore a suit. He looked so handsome. I thought it was sweet but that's how he was raised and, for him, the right thing to do. We did Easter with his parents, Thanksgiving at my house, then on Christmas he would go to church and lunch with his family then come over for dinner Christmas night. Mimi dog would hang on the front porch and wait for his dinner plate too.

***

After the shooting, he had been classified as partially disabled. He had nothing in the material sense, but he had everything as a human being. I often wondered what fully disabled looked like as I watched him do things that obviously hurt him a lot, as he worked to survive each day. He had severe rheumatoid arthritis, an after-effect of his multiple wounds, and was in constant pain. That's why he wore the coveralls, to keep his body as warm as he could. He had horrid scars and pucker marks from the wounds. He called them his zippers.

***

I was doing a lot of things when I lived in the neighborhood. I had three antique shops and the cafe, which was only open on the weekends. As I ran around getting different things done, I used to drag him with me. I had a small SUV and we were pilot and co-pilot. He didn't leave the neighborhood too much anymore. His piece of shit car had finally given up and, for the most part, riding the bus was a pain for him, both physically and in the general sense. We shopped, he went to auctions with me, to the post office to ship stuff, to drop off food at caterings. All over the place. We had so much fun.

He would tell me stories about the history and people of every neighborhood and area we drove through. It seemed that not only did he know ours, he knew many of the other areas almost as well too. I learned more from him than anyone there.

We were both early risers and I'd often find him in the mornings walking the streets with a giant clear plastic bag. The first time I asked him what the hell and he just laughed. He would walk and pick up cans to get money to eat and stay warm. He always joked that it was a good thing that the brothers liked The Bull. Then he'd keep going. I used to take him to the recycle place to cash them in. We'd put those jumbo bags in the back of the SUV, then off we'd go. That was fun too.

***

He was a proud man and a tough one too. He would never ask for anything nor would he complain about his life. I knew when it was bad though. You could see it. When I would mow my lawn, I'd just continue down and mow his too. When I bought food for my dogs, I would just buy a bag for him and drop it on the porch. I never said anything about it. It was the right thing to do. My fun with that was the one thing he really enjoyed was Heineken. He had grown to love it somewhere he was stationed and it was his happy place. He couldn't afford it very often, but every once in a while, he'd splurge and buy one bottle. I'm sure the memories are what made him smile. Turns out that every once in a while, the dog food fairy would also leave a six pack. It was magical.

***

I left there about a year after we met but would always pop by and check in with him as I passed through Virginia. This past June when I did, I only found his younger brother. He told me that he had passed away only two months before. That heart, that was so big and giving, finally gave out.

My Thoughts and Views

I have absolutely no impartiality when talking about him nor should I. If you've ever had a thought about how horrible your life or circumstance is, all you would have to do is spend a day with him. I learned so much about so much. I already understood forgiveness and I got to see that in action. I learned more about really seeing someone. I understood more about self-determination, outlook, acceptance of what is, and attitude. I allowed more compassion than cynicism. I learned to truly experience joy in the smallest moment. I learned how to love someone as a friend. And that's what he was. For that brief period in our lives, we were best friends.

<u>The Fallen Angel</u>

If you didn't know her, you might see a woman most likely in her early sixties who looks very sick and not long for this world. She's probably had a hard life. It looks like she did anyway. The truth is that she is a woman who did the best she could each day. A woman who is now at peace.

***

As part of my book tour this past summer, I went through my hometown. Even though it's been years since I lived there, I love the place. It's truly beautiful and has so many areas to just sit, relax, and be near the water. I had been running around all week and one day I was near one of my favorite little pocket parks. I decided to stop, sit on a bench by the water for a little while, and take a deep breath or two.

As I picked my bench and sat down, one over, there was a woman in my age range sitting in a wheelchair and enjoying the fresh air. She looked unwell. There was a younger man sitting on the bench beside her and talking quietly. I sat quiet at first though I kept looking their way. There was just something about her. As it sunk in, I got chills. I knew her. I knew it. She was my first love. She was the woman who had once saved my life. The odds of this happening had to be ridiculous, but there had to be a reason that it had. I got up my courage, stood up, and took the couple steps toward them. I smiled at the young man then squatted down beside her. I said, "_______, is that you, baby? It's me, Pam." Her breath caught, and tears ran down her face as she reached out a very feeble hand. I took it and held on as tears ran down my face as well.

*****

***

She grew up on the northeast side of town in a regular, middle-class world. Her mother was a homemaker and her father worked for the city. She had a brother five years older than her and though they loved each other, their age disparity made them not particularly close. She loved her mother too. She was a kind woman. But she was daddy's girl. Hard-headed and obstinate, they acted just alike though she looked like her mother.

She grew up in the late sixties and seventies, a time of turmoil everywhere. She was generally a good kid, but her curiosity often led her astray as she just had to see what was going on. Whatever that happened to be.

Her school career was average. She did okay but didn't stand out. By junior high, she was smoking pot. Not a big deal, everybody did it. But she fell into the other habits associated. Skipping class, lying to her parents, grades dropping. Her father and she began to butt heads often. She remembered fierce arguments that often scared her mother. But she'd go toe-to-toe with him. She wouldn't back down and neither would he.

By high school she was hanging with the stoner crowd though she was still hanging with school too. Mostly. She also began experimenting with harder drugs, they were so easy to get ahold of then.

The summer between eleventh and twelfth grade was her watershed period. She smoked heroin, it had been laced in a joint, for the first time, And, she got pregnant. She never went back to school.

***

Cutting back some, but not stopping, she continued to get high while pregnant. She said that she was punishing herself though at the time she didn't understand why. Her son was born six weeks premature. By the time he was home from the hospital, she was running the streets again.

Her life got even wilder and her parents did what they thought was best for everyone. They took custody of her son and kicked her out of the house. Not long after, she shot heroin for the first time with the guy that was her son's father.

Her next four years were mostly a blur.

At the end of that period, she went to rehab and got off heroin. With her parents support, she made it. She moved back in with them when she completed the program and worked to build a relationship with her little boy. He always knew she was his mom, but she was like an ethereal being to him, flitting in and out of his life. He loved her and feared her. His grandparents were the ones he could depend on.

As she got stronger, she got another waitress job and found a little Levittown house on a hippie cul-de-sac. She was still smoking pot, but she also started popping pills. No longer hypnotized by the needle, she stayed far away from that. But anything else was fair game.

I met her about a year later when I came to work in the same restaurant. There was something about her that made you care. She was just a very sweet person. Unless you got her fired up. That was always fun to watch.

She was about eight-and-a-half years older than me. When we met, I was fifteen and she was twenty-four. I had life traumas of my own though I didn't talk about any of it to anyone. Except her. As I said, there was something about her. And that something is what made me trust her. Over the next few months, she would get more upset and more upset by the things I told her. She really would have gone and kicked some butt for me. It all came to a head about six months after we met. I'd had a most terrible night but still showed for work. It's funny, her and I still remembered it the exact same. She said, "Fuck it. That's it. You're moving in with me." That is the day she saved my life. I've never forgotten. It was March 1979.

***

Back in the now, as our tears stopped, she fell into a light sleep. Without letting go of hers, I reached out my other hand to her son. As I shook his, I said, "________, you probably don't remember me. I think the last time I saw you was when you were nine." He gave a slight smile and began talking quietly. He did remember. He said he just vaguely remembers that when he was around six, his mother started calming some and began making a point to spend more time with him. He said that he remembered a girl coming with her most of the time. That girl was me.

I asked what was going on and he told me that she was terminally ill with the last stages of cervical cancer. She had found out she was HIV positive in the early nineties and over the years had gone up and down with it some, but it was finally going to beat her. His eyes watered as he told me that she was in Hospice care just up the road, but she had wanted to be outside near water and this park was the closest, so he'd brought her here. He really wasn't supposed to, but he thought that was stupid. She was dying and if she wanted to sit by water then he was going to make sure she did.

We sat and talked quietly about his life. He was cute now, but he was when he was little too. He was a cross between a hippie and a nerd. Of course, so am I. He is now forty-five which, to me, is kind of funny. He was born when she was so young, that he is only ten years younger than me.

He said that throughout his younger years, she was still that faraway goddess. They never lived together as mother and son. He lived his entire early life with his grandparents. I smiled and told him I remembered his grandfather's pride and joy, his candy apple red, vintage Ford pickup. He nodded and told me he had always loved riding in it. I asked after them then. He said his grandfather had passed away almost thirteen years before, when he was seventy-five. He told me that he was still the same throughout, always a gruff guy with a heart of gold, and that he still missed him. I shared a few memories I had, and he laughed. He said he always remembered her, pointing at his mother, and his grandfather butting heads. He said that never stopped, it was just the relationship they had, and over the years, it didn't really matter the topic, it continued much the same. I smiled as I had gotten to see a few of those. I asked about his grandmother and he said she had died just the year before at age eighty-seven. After his grandfather had died, she had moved into one of those senior places and stayed busy with activities and whatnot. I told him that she had always been very kind to me though it had to have been an odd situation for her. I asked about his uncle and he said that he had moved out west when he was young, and they'd had little to no contact over the years. He wasn't sure where he was now.

I then asked him about what he was up to and he said he lived in his grandparent's house still. They had given it to him. He added that after high school he had gone to the local university and was now a full-time geek. I told him that was pretty awesome and looked at his mom and said, "I know she's proud of who you are. She always was. Even when you were young, she thought you were just a cool person. That, I remember." He smiled and thanked me and then added, "I think I need to wake her up and get her back now."

When he had, she seemed disoriented at first. When she focused back in, she looked at me and whispered, "Will you stay with me?" I leaned and kissed her cheek, and answered, "Baby, I wouldn't be anywhere else."

***

As I got in my car to follow them to the Hospice, I turned off my phone. The woman in the car in front of me had saved my life and shared three years of hers with me. I was surely going to give her however much time she needed now. I loved her still. As I drove on, my mind wandered back to all those years ago.

When we got to the place and got her settled, she was soon asleep again. Her son asked if I minded if he went and got something to eat that wasn't Hospice food. I told him to go ahead, we'd be fine. When he left, I reached and took her hand, leaned back in the chair, and closed my eyes. Lost in thought.

A little later, I heard a whisper of a voice. "I can't believe it's you. That you're here. I never thought I'd see you again." I told her that though I'd never forgotten her for a minute, and shared our story often, that I never imagined I'd find her. And I was so glad that I had. She answered, "Almost too late." I squeezed her hand and told her I was just glad that I was here now and that was all that mattered. She asked if I had continued to travel the world. When I had gone away, that was my plan. As I continued to hold her hand, I filled her in on my life over the last thirty-six years. Her eyes were tearing again as she said, "I love you. I always have." She was soon asleep again.

Her son came back a few minutes later and sat down. I caught him up on our status then asked more about him. As he filled me in on his world, I told him I knew a kid now, even with the same name, that reminded me of him when he was young. He smiled, and we talked about that for a while. Then he asked if I was staying. I told him I was here for the duration. He had a sad look and said, "You know, she's always loved you. She talked about you now and then throughout the years. I didn't really remember until I saw you. I know she's glad you're here. Maybe she'll let go now." Both of our eyes teared as that came out of his mouth. After a few minutes he asked if I thought it was okay if he went home for a while. I told him most definitely and added that unfortunately the world didn't stop. I told him I'd be right here. He reached and brushed back her hair, whispered his thanks, and left.

I had my eyes closed again when she whispered out, "Will you lay here with me?" I squeezed her hand and got up. It was her turn to tell me about her last thirty-six years.

She said that soon after I went away, she had fallen in hard and kind of lost herself in the drug world. Everyone around her was doing the same and no one tried to stop her. She was dealing, she was doing, and in the end, she went back to the needle.

She said she'd had various short-term and no-term relationships. All unhealthy. She said that sometimes in her mellow times, she would think about me and wonder how and where I was. As she shared her darkest days, my eyes were tearing. She sounded like she'd been so lost. And for a long time. I asked how she'd made it through and she told me that like it had been for me in my early life, it was music that often kept her going, and talked about who, what, and how as she fell back into sleep. I petted her hair as she did.

She woke up after a few minutes and we talked more about that time, then she quieted again, and I said, "You were my first love, you know. I've never forgotten. Not a day goes by that I don't remember. If it wasn't for you, I wouldn't be here now." We were laying with me holding her as close as I could without hurting her. She whispered, "I think you were my only one." Quiet for a while again, I asked her what had happened. She said in 1992 she had gotten really sick, which wasn't a surprise because by then she was a strung-out junkie, but she had to go to the emergency room. Through a series of tests, it came back that she was HIV-positive. And she was devastated.

As she composed herself, I told her that was the year my father finally died and told her how he had. She smiled just a little and whispered, "Good." Her eyes closed for a little while and when she woke again, she started telling me what it had been like, how she'd felt, and just how terrified she was. She said she'd never really had to take responsibility for her choices, but they were going to end up costing her life instead. I held her closer as we both fell into sleep.

When I woke up next, it was daylight again. As I got up, I realized her son was there. I asked if all was okay, and he said he wasn't being weird or anything, but he had been there for a while and how nice it was that his mom got to be happy for a little while. I told him that he'd always given her that then I squeezed his shoulder and walked around in circles to stretch out some. He asked if it was okay if he left again. She was safe now and being taken care of and he was behind. I know he was having a very hard time and I asked him how long he had been there. He told me a week. We decided he'd stay until she woke up, spend some time with her, and let her know what he was doing, then he'd go.

He ended up staying through lunch and then I assumed my spot, holding her close, and talking to her quietly about the girls we once were and the women we were now. She was in and out of sleep all day and evening.

Very late, she woke up a little renewed. She whispered, "Will you dance with me? Like the night of your prom?" I told her I would love to. I got up carefully then got my laptop out and on and found what I remembered was her favorite. I got her up and said, "Ready, beautiful?" She nodded. Before I turned it on, I spoke and reassured her, "Everything is okay, baby. Let go of the pain, let go of the illness, let go of the hurt and worry. Just feel the music. I love you so much." I reached and started the music. When 'Gold Dust Woman' started, she whispered, "You remember." I answered, "Every minute." We danced, with me holding her up, so slow and gentle. We danced our last dance. Our bodies were in her room in the Hospice, but we were only in the music.

When I'd left her the first time, at the age of eighteen, to go see the world, I was devastated. Now she was leaving me, and I was again. We were both crying.

As we got back to the bed, I whispered, "Are you ready to go now, baby? It's okay if you are." In barely a whisper, she said, "I think I'm scared. I don't know what's going to happen. I'm so tired." My eyes were still tearing as I said, "I don't know either, baby. Nobody does. Just know that you are loved and safe. You won't feel pain anymore, only that. I'll always love you. That's a promise." I kissed her softly as she fell into sleep. I never did.

Three or four hours later, I'm not sure of the time, I felt her leave me. I can't even verbalize how it felt but I was in awe. I laid there with her for I'm not sure how long before I got up to go inform the staff.

She had been right. I'd found her just in time.

My Thoughts and Views

No matter the choices and decisions she made in life, she was intrinsically a good person. I knew it from the start. At a time in her life that was often tumultuous, she reached out to a young girl that needed help. When I say she saved my life, it's not a euphemism nor melodramatic, she truly did. Without that hand, I would not be here today.

The chance occurrence that I found her in the park that day can't be explained. Ever. I'll just say it was both right and meant to be that we were each there for the other when it really mattered.

When I told her I thought of her often, that is the truth. I loved her then. I love her still. Goodness always shines through. She was my hero, she was my champion, she was my lover, she was my friend. She was my angel.